Fool-Proofing Your Life

How to Deal Effectively with the Impossible People in Your Life

Jan Silvious

WATERBROOK
PRESS

P9-DBY-959

FOOLPROOFING YOUR LIFE
PUBLISHED BY WATERBROOK PRESS
12265 Oracle Boulevard, Suite 200
Colorado Springs, Colorado 80921

Unless otherwise noted, Scriptures are from The Holy Bible,
New International Version, copyright © 1973, 1984 by International
Bible Society, used by permission of Zondervan Publishing House.
Also quoted is The New American Standard Bible (NASB), copyright
© The Lockman Foundation, 1960, 1962, 1963, 1968, 1971, 1972,
1973, 1975, 1977. Used by permission, all rights reserved.

Details in some anecdotes and stories have been changed
to protect the identities of the persons involved.

ISBN: 978-0-307-45848-3

Published in the United States by WaterBrook Multnomah, an imprint
of the Crown Publishing Group, a division of Random House Inc.,
New York.

WATERBROOK and its deer colophon are registered trademarks of
Random House Inc.

Printed in the United States of America
2009

10 9 8 7 6 5 4 3 2 1

SPECIAL SALES
Most WaterBrook Multnomah books are available at special quantity discounts when
purchased in bulk by corporations, organizations, and special-interest groups. Custom
imprinting or excerpting can also be done to fit special needs. For information, please
e-mail SpecialMarkets@WaterBrookMultnomah.com or call 1-800-603-7051.

TO LAUREN

Keep sound wisdom and discretion,
So they will be life to your soul,
And adornment to your neck.
Then you will walk in your way securely,
And your foot will not stumble.
When you lie down, you will not be afraid;
When you lie down, your sleep will be sweet.
Do not be afraid of sudden fear,
Nor of the onslaught of the wicked when it comes;
For the LORD will be your confidence,
And will keep your foot from being caught.

—PROVERBS 3:21-26, NASB

CONTENTS

FOREWORD

How fortunate is the one blessed with the company of wise and fun-loving companions! For over twenty-five years, since the first Precept Bible studies began, God has blessed my life richly and abundantly through my friendship with Jan Silvious. During that time, not only have we raised our sons together, but we've laughed (with Jan, you can't help but laugh), cried, prayed, ministered, but most importantly, studied God's Word together. I have watched her mature into the wonderful and wise woman of God she is today... and she has watched me mature. We've grown together.

This is a woman I know, and there are so many reasons to admire and respect my friend. Many people know Jan as my able co-host on Precept Ministries' national radio program, *Precept Live with Kay and Jan.* Others recognize her as a popular conference speaker, author, or guest host on the national radio programs *Mid-Day Connection* and *Open Line.* Still others know her on a more intimate, personal level as an experienced and gifted counselor.

In each of these areas, Jan has demonstrated a unique ability to help men and women find practical applications for dealing with real-life issues. She sees matters clearly, and she is skilled at putting them into perspective. Yet her "straight talk" is wonderfully palatable, often tempered with perfectly timed humor and always marked by unconditional love. When Jan speaks, one truly wants to hear what she has to say. She is one amazing woman.

None of this, however, explains what I love most dearly about Jan Silvious. That she is an excellent writer, a fine counselor, and an accomplished speaker cannot be denied. What makes her unique—what draws me to her again and again—is her high regard for Scripture, her unwavering passion for pursuing biblical wisdom, and her determination to apply God's truths to even the most confounding circumstances of life. And her delightful perspective gives hope, even to those in dire circumstances. It's a kind of godly c'est la vie—such is life! These are the qualities that make her the covenant friend I so love and admire.

Perhaps, like me, you have listened in awe as Jan speaks on our Sunday night call-in program. During such times, and throughout the years of our friendship, Jan has taught me much about life, about people . . . about wisdom.

She'll teach you, too, if you are but willing to learn, beloved.

Take what Jan says, as we teach people to do, to the plumb line of God's Word—and then do accordingly.

KAY ARTHUR
CHATTANOOGA, TN

ACKNOWLEDGMENTS

Thank you is in order for some special people who have walked through the book-writing process with me. Some were there early on to encourage me, and some have come lately to cheer me across the finish line. To each of you, I am grateful.

To the Group: You know who you are, you know where we have been, and you know what God has done.

To Debra: You cheered me on while the book languished and then came to life.

To Sandy: You were a faithful encourager from the beginning.

To Debbie: You went "Home" before the book came out, but you cheered me on until the day you died!

To Mark: You draw word pictures like no other. I have learned much.

To Rebecca: Without your belief, this book would not be.

To Traci: Your touch on the words has been full of grace, and your spirit has been gentle and kind.

To Mother: You did a lot of "foolproofing" when I was a youngster, and I am grateful.

To my family—Charlie, David, Sandi, Lauren, Jon, Aaron, and Heather: Each of you is a delight to my soul!

To all of you who have asked, "How's the book?" Here it is. Your interest has kept me writing for a very long time!

PART 1

Is There a Fool
in Your Life?

Know that wisdom is thus for your soul;
If you find it, then there will be a future,
And your hope will not be cut off.

PROVERBS 24:14, NASB

We have no words for speaking of wisdom to the stupid
He who understands the wise is wise already.

G. C. LICHTENBERG

Nine-tenths of wisdom consists in being wise in time.

THEODORE ROOSEVELT

The wise man is also the just, the pious, the upright,
the man who walks in the way of truth.

OTTO ZUCKLER

CHAPTER ONE

Raising Your Relational IQ

Sally looked wistfully at the other women in the room. She had come to the Christmas party at church reluctantly, hoping to find some peace and joy for her soul. But in the midst of her friends' amiable banter, all she could hear were the words of her husband, Don. They were words that had cut her to the quick: "You are so dull and stupid. I don't know why I ever married you."

Don was on one of his tears. Just last month he seemed to be doing better, trying harder and treating his wife better, but then things began to tense up. There had been a minor disagreement over a Christmas present, and from that point on, Don had seemed to become angrier and angrier. The man who just a few days before had vowed his love for her now was cursing her and raging at her. This man she loved but feared was almost destroying her.

It was so hard to put it all together. Her pensive look would have given her away if anyone had looked at her closely. Although she was among women who loved her and wanted to include her, she was on an island in her mind, trying to figure out why she felt so crazy.

Maybe you are like Sally. You understand what it means to be caught in the undertow of a relationship that seems to pull you down. Each time there is a lull in the tension, you tell yourself, *This time, everything is going to be all right.* Yet in a few hours or a few days, you are thrust into confusion again. Often you are blamed for whatever negative circumstances occur, and yet for the life of you you can't figure out why.

Sarah is a woman who was forced to look reality square in the face. "My mother can be so much fun and a real friend in tough situations, if she wants to be. She is generous with my kids, and we look forward to her monthly visits."

Sarah tried to love her mother, Mary, but Mary had another side to her that baffled Sarah and everyone else. "I guess you could say she has a major blind spot," Sarah explained. "Everything will be going along fine, and then something happens to upset Mother. We never know what it will be, we just find out that she's upset. Her anger flares, and she has what my dad always called 'one of her three-day mad spells.'

"She's had these so many times throughout my life that I have felt there was no hope. I've figured that's just the way she is and I just have to live with her spells that throw us all off balance. What bothers me now, however, is that I've seen her do the same thing to my children. She tells them, 'If you don't want to come stay with Granny, it's okay,' but then she punishes them for not coming. She withdraws, and no one hears from her until she eventually calls. Then everything is fine again—for a while."

Sarah's eyes filled with tears as she recalled a particularly painful incident with her mother. "My daughter had a very rare form of cancer three years ago, when she was eight. Since my mother lives only an hour from us, she volunteered to stay at the house with my son while my husband and I were at the hospital. The afternoon after Mother arrived, she called the hospital room, demanding to know where I 'hid' the mop. She wanted to clean my 'filthy' kitchen floor. Since we were talking to the oncologist about the treatment plan for my daughter, I told Mother I would have to call her back. She insisted that I tell her right then where I put the mop! Sensing by my end of the conversation that she was pushing me, my husband took the phone and said, 'Mary, we will call you back later. The doctor is here, and we can't talk.' Then he just hung up the phone.

"When we got home that evening, Mother wasn't speaking. She never asked about her granddaughter but only made an announcement: 'I am leaving.' I was too exhausted from the whole ordeal with my daughter to argue with her, so I just went to the bedroom and closed the door. I heard Mother say one last loud sentence to my husband before the front door slammed. 'Obviously,' she said, 'my presence isn't needed.' I didn't have the energy to stop her, and honestly, I didn't want to try. We had been through episodes like this before. I always found a way to smooth things over, to pack it all away and never mention it again until finally things would return to normal…if you can call that kind of relationship normal.

"About three days later, Mother called and asked about my little girl as if she hadn't even been at our house. I was angry with her, but as usual, I told her what she wanted to hear, and I never brought up the incident again. There have been other incidents since then, and they're really starting to wear me out. My dad tried to reason with her for years about her 'mad spells,' but he might as well have been talking to the wall. She refuses to even admit she has them much less be willing to change. She thinks she is just fine, and if people have a problem with her, well, it's just too bad. They are wrong, and if she's really mad, she calls them 'stupid'!

"I love my mother, and I want to be a good daughter. I don't want to be mean or act unchristian, but I just can't stand to walk on eggshells anymore. And I don't want my children to have to either. Something's got to change…but I'm afraid it will never be Mother."

Sarah is describing the kind of complex, crazy-making relationship many of us experience sometime in our lives. Her mother, as generous and fun as she can sometimes be, has more than a blind spot. She has a dangerous character flaw that ensures that anyone who gets close to her will eventually be ensnared by her manipulation. Mary exhibits the behavior of one whom the Bible identifies as a *fool*. The reality is, relating to her will always involve emotional chaos.

HOPELESSLY ENTANGLED

If you've had a relationship like Sally's or Sarah's, you know how conflicted it makes you feel. You love but you hate. You trust but you suspect. You enjoy but you want to get away. You understand but you just can't excuse. You embrace but you want to push back. You know you are needed but you feel abused.

You can't put your finger on the problem. You know there is one, but if you ever bring it up with the other person, very quickly it is turned into something that is all about you and what you've done. You are told in so many words, "If you were different, there wouldn't be a problem." Your accuser works to produce guilt in you and evoke pity for himself. You are left to ponder, *What can I do to make this better? I must be doing something very wrong.*

Over the years, I have talked to so many people entangled in this kind of relationship. Usually they are quite candid about their own faults. They chew their fingernails or tap their feet while telling me, "I am willing to correct what I can, but for the life of me, I don't know what to do." They remain baffled because no matter what they do to alter their shortcomings, the relationship stays chaotic and tense. Often they assume they're the only one in the world with a relationship that is so insane! They feel like a wart growing on the face of a smooth-complected society. They don't want to talk about the pain because they have been told so often that they are the reason for it. They have almost come to believe it. Since they care about the difficult individual, they feel like a betrayer to mention the problem to anyone. So they keep on keeping on in hopeful desperation, always believing things will be better tomorrow. But when their tomorrow comes, they are usually disappointed.

My heart hurts for you if you are in this kind of situation. I know how it leaves you crushed in spirit although you look intact on the outside. These things I know about you because the symptoms of a person entangled with a fool are fairly universal:

- You can't figure out why this relationship just can't work.
- You fear losing what you think you have with this person, whatever that might be (you may not be able to define it!).
- You feel guilty for failing to find a solution to the ongoing pain.
- You are afraid to face the truth and possible consequences. The unknown is very threatening to you.
- You know you have to do something to change the destructive dynamics, but you don't know what you need to do.

The reason you remain in turmoil is that you are trying to relate to someone who has some wonderful qualities mixed with a perplexing set of destructive characteristics. In the beginning you may have admired this person, but soon you found yourself mired in the chaos that seems to characterize the relationship. One minute you hear your own laughter, and you hope against hope that all is well. The next minute you're on the defensive in response to some inane comment or emotional jab made at you by this one to whom you are trying to relate. If you protest, invariably the person denies he has said or done anything inappropriate. In a few twists of the facts, he tries to convince you that you're a bitter person or just "oversensitive." When you have been labeled with all other conceivable insults, there sometimes comes the appellation you hate more than any other: "crazy." It leaves you bleeding. What can you possibly do or say to counter that one? By the time the encounter is over, you are kicking yourself for even mentioning that you have feelings.

RELATIONAL INTELLIGENCE

The apostle Paul wrote to the believers in Rome with these instructions:

> Bless those who persecute you; bless and curse not. Rejoice with those who rejoice, and weep with those who weep. Be of the same mind toward one another; do not be haughty in mind, but associate with the lowly. Do not be wise in your own estimation. Never pay back evil for evil to anyone. Respect what is right in the sight of all men. If possible, so far as it depends on you, be at peace with all men. (Romans 12:14-18, NASB)

Peace with everyone surely is the goal for us as believers. But it is not always possible. When you encounter a situation that has a one-sided peace, then living with the fallout can leave you exhausted and bewildered.

Over the years I have spent many hours "riding the ambulance" with too many people who have been wounded (and sometimes "left for dead") by someone they loved or were tied to through blood. I have seen too many people locked in a grid of fright, guilt, and anger because of the "shoulds" and the "oughts" that have been used as weapons to force them into an uneasy peace. I have seen many of them turn to the church or to well-meaning, believing friends or relatives only to experience a total lack of understanding of what they are going through as they try to relate to a person who abhors peace. So often, the person who is doing the "trying" is the one who is blamed if peace doesn't work. This ought not to be!

Well over fifteen years ago I began to see patterns in the people who crossed my path as I spoke around the country and as I worked in a counseling office. Their symptoms were the same, and the "methods" used by their difficult person were the same. In each instance, with very little deviation, I saw a person who wanted a decent relationship living as a hostage of someone who was unwilling to take personal responsibility for his or her actions. I was amazed to note that it did not matter whether the hostage-taker was a mother, a husband, a child, a sister, a friend, or a boss; the behavior was the same, and the results were the same. One person held control and through open rage, passive anger, oily manipulation, or sullen silence stubbornly refused to release his grip.

It became more and more obvious to me that the people who consistently operated this way were in a category all their own, yet many Christians I talked with failed to see that the traditional, even biblical, way of handling most relational difficulties might need to be reexamined when this kind of person was part of the equation. They continued to bash their heads and hearts against the proverbial wall, hoping against hope that this time things would be different.

Witnessing so much suffering, often in the name of Christian love, inspired me to become a champion for those in impossible relationships. I began to search the Scriptures and reason with the Lord. This book is a result of my impassioned quest. When I began to see the behavior and mind-set of the difficult person I was encountering or hearing about clearly described in the book of Proverbs, I thought, *This is it!* God knew there would be people who would be "right in their own eyes" (Proverbs 12:15, NASB) and who would freely speak their minds without any regard for the consequences. He knew and declared that there would be people who would be dangerous to embrace. God knew there would be those to whom you could not entrust yourself, so he offered an alternative way of behaving with these particular people. Nowhere did he exempt us from the call to forgiveness or love, but he did issue warning upon warning that, if heeded, would liberate the captive from the hostage-taker…the victim from the victimizer…the wise from the foolish.

If you feel entangled in a relationship that is difficult, confusing, crazy-making, and often painful, my passion is to offer you hope for a better way to live—a way that honors God and yet is free from the often tyrannical nature of the difficult person in your life.

I can tell you from extensive experience in working with people ensnared in relationships with fools that becoming disentangled requires extraordinary discernment and God-given wisdom. You may not immediately recognize when you're dealing with a fool, but when an ordinary relational predicament turns into a morass of confusion and conflict, you need to consider the possibility that the skills that work for most relationships just won't work in this one. You must master an alternative set of relational skills if you want to survive the relationship. It is relational suicide to assume you can win over a fool by argument, sweet reasonableness, or any other common wisdom. Even the Christian virtues like gentleness, patience, and turning the other cheek may only get you in a deeper mess. To relate to a fool takes an uncommon prudence that can be gleaned only by those who truly desire it. I call that wisdom "relational intelligence."

Why not test your own relational intelligence by taking the fol[l]-ing little quiz? Answer yes or no to the questions, then we'll take a loo[k] at what your own answers tell us.

Yes No

❏ ❏ Do you feel your difficult person is displeased with you most of the time?

❏ ❏ Do you feel responsible for "clearing things up" with your difficult person?

❏ ❏ Are you surprised when your difficult person is upset with you or with a particular circumstance that involves you?

❏ ❏ Does the upset often come "out of the blue"?

❏ ❏ Do you spend time devising remedies to make your difficult person happier?

❏ ❏ Do you believe that he or she is really a good person who is just "difficult to get along with" sometimes?

❏ ❏ When you feel your difficult person's anger, do you change the way you behave?

❏ ❏ Do you try to appease his or her anger?

❏ ❏ Do you argue with him or her?

❏ ❏ Does your difficult person define your life? Do you see yourself as the person your difficult person describes?

❏ ❏ Does he or she tell you what you should think about things in general and about yourself in particular?

❏ ❏ Do you ever think, *This isn't so bad?*

❏ ❏ Do you ever think, *If I would be different, he or she would change?*

If you have answered yes to as many as five of these questions, then it's possible you haven't yet seen the other person for who he or she really realize where such a relationship inevitably leads. ... ational IQ, you will mistakenly believe that the ...y in normal relationships can be applied in this one. ...y waste many precious years making the same mistakes over and over, ending up extremely frustrated and hurt. I think this tendency is the part of this whole problem that bothers me the most: the wasted years that could have been full and rich. But because of the relational entanglement, days and months seem to slip away without anything to show for "the living"—except confusion and strife and an abundance of graying hair.

I encourage you to be absolutely honest with yourself for a moment. Have you tried everything you can think of to untangle the relationship that causes you the most difficulty? If you're anything like Sally or Sarah, you have experimented with new relational skills and hunted for effective scriptural principles. You may even have three-by-five cards taped all over your bathroom mirror that highlight scriptures to which you are clinging for survival. You have blamed yourself more times than you care to remember and have tried to change the way you behave so the person you're relating to sees the change and alters his own behavior. You have tried to "let go and let God." (Let God do *what*, you're not sure, but sometimes you just need the relief of letting go!) When the good days come, you sigh with relief. *Everything is going to be all right!* Things seem to go back to normal, and you can remember why you love this person, why you want this connection to work, and why it's important to you.

Then it happens. You are thrown off balance by your difficult person's words or behavior, and you relearn the hard lesson that's inevitably learned by everyone who tries to get close to a fool: To love a fool is like hugging a fan; you will only be sliced up in the process.

Do You Love a Fool?

You probably aren't ready to boldly proclaim that someone you love is a fool. But perhaps you're at least ready to investigate the possibility that you're in a situation that needs to be marked SPECIAL HANDLING! *Fool* is not a pretty word, and you may hesitate to apply it to anyone you know. If you have ever read Jesus' warning in Matthew 5:20-22, then your hesitancy is certainly understandable:

> For I tell you that unless your righteousness surpasses that of the Pharisees and the teachers of the law, you will certainly not enter the kingdom of heaven. You have heard that it was said to the people long ago, "Do not murder, and anyone who murders will be subject to judgment." But I tell you that anyone who is angry with his brother will be subject to judgment. Again, anyone who says to his brother, "Raca," is answerable to the Sanhedrin. But anyone who says, "You fool!" will be in danger of the fire of hell.

Those are heavy words. Any intelligent person would want to think twice before uttering that four-letter word, *fool*. But are these words of Jesus encouraging you to put your head in the sand while ignoring foolish behavior? Or might he instead be warning against labeling someone a fool because you are angry and it seems like a good epithet to use? Could he be saying, "Don't label someone a fool because you dislike him. That is destructive"? "Man's anger," according to James 1:20, never works the righteousness of God. So to use your anger to bring about a change in your fool only puts you in the same category your fool occupies. God does not condone such self-protective behavior. But he does call us to truthfulness. The Lord never skirted truth nor backed away from it. He always moved with great compassion and tenderness, but he never denied reality. If you want to untangle the difficult situation in which you may find yourself, it is important for you to be courageous enough to face the truth and seek the wisdom you will need to make the next move.

It's hard, isn't it, to face reality? I understand. We always want things to be better than they are. We try to convince ourselves, *She's just moody.* Or, *He had a bad childhood, so of course he rages!* You may think, *If I were a different sort of person, maybe we could make this whole thing work. If I had a different personality or if I were more caring…* But if the truth of the matter is that you are caught in a fool's web, then you can't just wait and hope things will change.

In Scripture the word *fool* is used frequently and pointedly, and specific guidance is given on what to do about a person who thinks foolishly and therefore practices foolish behavior. So, to identify an individual as a fool and to respond to him accordingly does not put you in danger of hellfire. Rather, it gives you intelligent information in regard to the kind of person he or she is and what behavior you can consistently expect. To lack this consciousness will leave you relationally handicapped and vulnerable to a great deal of unnecessary pain.

In order to foolproof your life, you will need the wisdom of God, just as King Solomon did. Solomon was appointed to rule over the nation of Israel as successor to his father, the beloved King David. The job was incredibly complex, and Solomon knew he needed divine guidance. Recognizing the limited scope of his own relational intelligence, he went to the Lord and said, "So give your servant a discerning heart to govern your people and to distinguish between right and wrong. For who is able to govern this great people of yours?" (1 Kings 3:9).

God answered Solomon's prayer. "God gave Solomon wisdom and

very great insight, and a breadth of understanding as measureless as the sand on the seashore. Solomon's wisdom was greater than the wisdom of all the men of the East, and greater than all the wisdom of Egypt" (1 Kings 4:29-30).

Proverbs 3:13-18 says,

Blessed is the man who finds wisdom,
  the man who gains understanding,
for she is more profitable than silver
  and yields better returns than gold.
She is more precious than rubies;
  nothing you desire can compare with her.
Long life is in her right hand;
  in her left hand are riches and honor.
Her ways are pleasant ways,
  and all her paths are peace.
She is a tree of life to those who embrace her;
  those who lay hold of her will be blessed.

The book of Proverbs is the place where uncommon wisdom is spelled out in a very common way. It is for people who want to know the truth and who are willing to take it at face value. It is packed with the kind of wisdom we need to deal with our most difficult entanglements. Let's look more closely at what it has to say about the fools we love or think we should.

The first step in foolproofing your life is to take an honest look at your current relationships and the way you feel and behave in them. Unless you can "raise your relational IQ," you may repeat destructive patterns and stay entangled in unpleasant dynamics without even realizing you have a part to play.

Let's begin our journey toward higher relational intelligence (and greater wisdom, peace, and joy) by considering the truth (and nothing but the truth) about our most important relationships.

Think About It

1. Spend some quiet time alone and evaluate your significant relationships as honestly as you can. Are there any that are particularly difficult? If so, which one(s)?

2. What feelings surface as you contemplate your relationship with this difficult person?

3. Is the concept of being caught in the undertow of a relationship a reality for you? Try to describe some of the reasons why.

4. Consider the following characteristics of a relationship with a fool, and check as many as are true for you in your difficult relationship:
   - chaotic ups and downs
   - periods of extreme emotional and relational tension
   - walking on eggshells
   - confusion
   - desperation
   - despair
   - fear
   - guilt
   - being blamed for whatever is "wrong"
   - blaming yourself for your difficult person's behavior
   - feeling crazy
   - feeling off balance
   - feeling like a hostage
   - feeling manipulated
   - feeling controlled

5. List your difficult person's "good" qualities—the things that draw you to him or her or give you hope for the relationship.

6. List your difficult person's "bad" qualities—the things that make you wonder if you can survive the relationship and that convince you that your "relational intelligence" needs a boost.

7. Think about specific ways you have tried to untangle your difficult relationship or change the painful dynamic. List as many of your strategies as you can recall.

8. Have any of them worked—even in the short term? Why or why not?

9. List any "excuses" you have made for your difficult person. Consider how excusing or justifying the foolish behavior has enabled you to stay tangled in an unhealthy relational dynamic.

10. Consider this statement: "To love a fool is like hugging a fan; you will only be sliced up in the process." Have you ever felt this way? If so, describe the circumstances.

Go to God About It

Looking deeply and honestly at our most difficult relationships can plunge us into confusion and despair pretty quickly if we forget God. If it's all up to us to figure out what to do, then we're in trouble! Fortunately, he doesn't leave us alone in our predicament. Rather, he brings us the "precious rubies" of his wisdom and the pleasures of his peace (Proverbs 3:15,17) as we seek his guidance for our lives.

Spend a few minutes meditating on the passage that follows and consider God's faithful, powerful love for you as you begin the journey toward foolproofing your life.

Jeremiah 29:11-14

For I know the plans I have for you," declares the LORD, "plans to prosper you and not to harm you, plans to give you hope and a future. Then you will call upon me and come and pray to me, and I will listen to you. You will seek me and find me when you seek me with all your heart. I will be found by you," declares the LORD, "and will bring you back from captivity. I will gather you from all the nations and places where I have banished you," declares the LORD, "and will bring you back to the place from which I carried you into exile."

Consult the Bible About It

Wisdom is a wonderful attribute that offers you safety, protection, and insight. No one is born with wisdom, but it is given freely by the Lord to anyone who seeks it earnestly.

Consider the following scriptures and what they have to tell you about this precious commodity.

1. Where does wisdom begin? From where do you receive wisdom?

   Proverbs 1:7
   The fear of the LORD is the beginning of knowledge,
   > but fools despise wisdom and discipline.

   Proverbs 2:6
   For the LORD gives wisdom,
   > and from his mouth come knowledge and understanding.

   Proverbs 9:10
   The fear of the LORD is the beginning of wisdom,
   > and knowledge of the Holy One is understanding.

2. Why is wisdom so very important in your life?

   Proverbs 4:5-9
   Get wisdom, get understanding;
   > do not forget my words or swerve from them.

Do not forsake wisdom, and she will protect you;
　　love her, and she will watch over you.
Wisdom is supreme; therefore get wisdom.
　　Though it cost all you have, get understanding.
Esteem her, and she will exalt you;
　　embrace her, and she will honor you.
She will set a garland of grace on your head
　　and present you with a crown of splendor.

3. What will wisdom (relational intelligence) look like in your life?

Proverbs 11:2-3
When pride comes, then comes disgrace,
　　but with humility comes wisdom.
The integrity of the upright guides them,
　　but the unfaithful are destroyed by their duplicity.

Proverbs 14:33
Wisdom reposes in the heart of the discerning
　　and even among fools she lets herself be known.

Proverbs 24:14
Know also that wisdom is sweet to your soul;
　　if you find it, there is a future hope for you,
and your hope will not be cut off.

What Will You Do About It?

Write out a prayer of gratitude and faith (whether you feel them or not!), affirming your willingness to consider what God has to teach you about your difficult relationship, yourself, and his wisdom. Attach your prayer to the inside front cover of this book and pray it often in the days ahead. It is not easy to sort through the complex issues foolproofing your life will entail, but God is faithful! He will not abandon you anywhere on your journey. Practice placing all your hope in him, time after time, day after day. You will be glad you did.

You who are simple, gain prudence;
you who are foolish, gain understanding.

PROVERBS 8:5

The more intelligent a man is,
the more originality he discovers in men.
Ordinary people see no differences between men.

BLAISE PASCAL

A fool sees not the same tree that a wise man sees.

WILLIAM BLAKE

Fools rush in where Angels fear to tread.

ALEXANDER POPE

CHAPTER TWO

Flavors of Foolishness

Wherever I talk to a group about fools, inevitably I am asked, "Well, aren't we all fools?" When you consider the gene pool of humanity right now, you might think so, but the answer is no. We have all done foolish things, but we don't all qualify as fools, according to the biblical definition.

Occasional foolish behavior goes with being human. Foolish acts that we blunder into make up some of the scenery in all of our lives. Those events can be embarrassing to recall, but maturing individuals learn from their mistakes and are careful not to repeat their folly. Sometimes the cost of the folly is high, but the greater the expense the stronger the lesson in wisdom.

For example, as a newlywed I bought encyclopedias from some itinerant guys working our neighborhood. Their line was, "We will place these books in your home for free." I don't know how we got around to the 'free' encyclopedias costing six hundred dollars—but they did, and for months my young husband and I paid for those books that were virtually useless to us. That was thirty years ago, but we keep that set of antiquated books on a shelf in a closet. They are a good reminder of my folly. I learned the expensive way that you can't get anything for free.

I am older and wiser now, and while I still do foolish things, I can honestly say I have been more alert to potential folly since then. Foolish acts are common, but if we are fortunate, they don't cost us more than a few dollars, a little inconvenience, or a mild scare. We will act foolishly sometimes just because we are human. There is a group of people, however, who seem hard-pressed to learn the lessons that most of us learn when we do something unwise.

God knew that King Solomon would encounter foolish behavior as he was ruling Israel. He would find it in the people, but he would see it in himself as well. So, within the proverbs that are recorded in Scripture, there is an abundance of the wisdom the king gained in relating to fools. Solomon had a great nation to rule, and it was important for him to recognize those he could trust, those he should keep his eye on, and how to tell the difference.

In these scriptures there seem to be gradations of foolishness, so if you really want to understand your difficult relationship, it is important to gain insight into the kind of person to whom you are relating. Let's take a look at the different flavors of foolishness described in the book of Proverbs.

FOOLISH BY INCIDENT

Do you know someone who seems to make the same mistakes over and over but can't figure out why? She doesn't set out with any ill intent; she just does whatever seems right at the moment with no consideration for the possible consequences in her life or in anyone else's. In the book of Proverbs, this type of individual is referred to as *simple* (or *naive*). This does not mean *stupid;* it merely means "without insight." The root word in the Hebrew means "spacious, gullible, and open-minded" (not in a good sense). I think of these fools as people with a lot of air between their ears! This is a person who tends to believe anything she's told and who lives in denial of the consequences of her actions. She just bops along, letting her foolishness spill out incident by incident.

A naive (or simple) person runs on immediate feelings, not according to bottom-line facts. This is the woman who gets into a bad love relationship and, even if liberated at great cost, quickly hops into another, convincing herself, *This time, it's really love!* It's the man who seeks counsel for a while but rarely follows through with the help he is afforded. He may straighten up and fly right for a time, but he is just as likely to revert to his simple, nonintentional life.

Naive, simple people can be wise in some areas, even quite successful, but emotionally and spiritually they are dispossessed. I know some professional people who are brilliant in their fields. They make wise business choices, but when it comes to relationships, they are exceedingly naive and simple. They don't see where they're going and often get into trouble. The Scriptures make it clear that "A prudent man sees evil and hides himself, the naive proceed and pay the penalty" (Proverbs 27:12, NASB).

Lori divorced her husband, Michael, for his philandering ways. His frequent adulteries embarrassed and enraged her, so she quickly dispatched him. At a singles group within two months of the divorce, she met Ron, a soft-spoken charmer with a winning smile. Four months later they were married. "What's wrong with that?" you ask. Perhaps nothing, except that Ron's first wife had divorced him for having affairs. Lori knew that, but she could rationalize anything if it meant she could have what she wanted. She thought she wanted Ron because she was convinced, *He will change for me!* Obviously Lori is a simple, naive woman. She will probably be bitterly disappointed with her choice and pay a penalty of pain that would have been unnecessary if she had been wiser.

Simple people need a great deal of patient understanding. Sometimes they seem to be so outrageously optimistic about their own choices that they have trouble seeing the obvious pitfalls that a wiser person probably would recognize. It may take the rude awakening of seeing someone else in trouble for the simple person to actively seek wisdom and change. "When a mocker is punished, the simple gain wisdom" (Proverbs 21:11). Simple people *can* learn from others' mistakes—if you can get their attention.

Naive people can also learn from the consequences of their own folly, so just being patient while they limp along isn't always the answer. It could be that if naive people were allowed to pay the price for their folly every time, they would ultimately be corrected by the consequences just from the sheer fear of repeated discipline. That is not the ideal way to learn, but it is a way that seems to work—if anything will work—with the naive.

Jeff is a young man in his late twenties who has made many poor choices, and although he always talks a good game, he doesn't seem to learn from the pain he goes through. Now, however, he is beginning to make progress. For the first twenty-five years of his life his parents paid his bills, covered his debts, and basically kept the feathers in his nest clean and fluffy. But recently they told him, "This is it. You have made your last mess with our financial accounts." They firmly stuck to their decision, and after some creative negotiation with creditors, Jeff was able to keep his car and pay the rent on his little two-room house. His folks had been patient with their "little bird" until he had exhausted their resources. Then they finally (and wisely) saw that nothing they did in coming to his aid was going to change him. Reluctantly, but with great resolve, they moved from patiently waiting for things to change to a more assertive stance: They allowed Jeff's circumstances to discipline him. After a few months this naive young man began to learn that if he was going to have a car and a roof over his head, it was up to him. He wised up because his parents helped him grow up.

FOOLISH BY CHARACTER

The category of individual who is the lead character of this book never wises up. There are two scriptures in the Proverbs that describe him with a broad sweep.

> The way of a fool seems right to him,
>> but a wise man listens to advice.
>>> (Proverbs 12:15)

> A fool finds no pleasure in understanding
>> but delights in airing his own opinions.
>>> (Proverbs 18:2)

Fools think they are always right, and they like to speak their own minds. To cap off these descriptions, the Bible tells us that a fool's behavior is chronic.

> As a dog returns to its vomit,
>> so a fool repeats his folly.
>>> (Proverbs 26:11)

This bona fide fool can be a mother, father, husband, wife, son, daughter, brother, sister, in-law, friend, employer, employee, neighbor, or minister. According to Proverbs, a person who is a fool by character doesn't know he is a fool and has no clue about his impact on relationships.

In fact, he doesn't care, because he believes there is only one way to relate—his way. There is only one way to think in a relationship, and that is the way the fool thinks. A fool is closed to any suggestion that his thinking might be flawed or that his behavior might be inappropriate. If a fool's spouse is unhappy about something, then there is something wrong with the spouse. If a fool's children are struggling, the fool calls them "stupid." If a fool's boss corrects him, then the boss is "out of line" or "unfair." If the people who work for a fool are not producing what he wants, then they are labeled "lazy" and "no good."

Never can an accusation of any sort stick to a fool. Fools rebel against anyone who might dare to intervene in their lives and test their emotional or spiritual IQ. Because fools' ways are always right in their own eyes and because fools take pride in airing their own opinions, they never confess or repent. Why would they want to? They believe they are always right. This mind-set is at the very core of the fool's being, and it controls all he is and everything he does.

Three Hebrew words are used in Proverbs to describe this kind of individual. Each word reflects a slightly different aspect of the fool's character.

Closed-minded

The first word, *kesil*, means "a dull and closed mind." This aspect of the fool is demonstrated by thickheadedness and stubbornness. By his laziness and shortsightedness, this kind of individual rejects information and feedback from others. A *kesil* fool may be the lady next door—seemingly harmless but totally closed to what anyone might have to say. She is in her own world, and she doesn't want anyone to interfere.

The word *kesil* is used in Proverbs 15:14 (NASB): "The mind of the intelligent seeks knowledge, but the mouth of fools feeds on folly." Note there is no reference to this person using his mind. This fool's mouth is the weapon of choice, and folly is the ammunition. *Kesil* is translated "fool" forty-nine times in Proverbs, more than any other word for fool. When you begin to look around you, you see that closed-mindedness, thickheadedness, and stubbornness come in various shapes, colors, and genders. No matter what form this attitude takes, at the core of every certified fool you will find a mind closed to any information that might challenge his way of thinking.

Spiritually Bereft

A less frequently used Hebrew word for fool is *nabal*. It is used only three times in Proverbs and refers to one who lacks spiritual perception. Proverbs 30:21-24 gives insight into this fool's flavor: "Under three things the earth trembles, under four it cannot bear up: a servant who becomes king, a fool who is full of food, an unloved woman who is married, and a maidservant who displaces her mistress." If a fool's basic needs are satisfied, he rarely looks around to see if anyone else is in need or if more effort might be required of him. He is content, and that is enough.

Psalm 14:1 uses the word *nabal* as well: "The fool has said in his heart, 'There is no God'" (NASB). The fool may not come right out and say that, but by showing a self-protective attitude that says, "I will meet my own needs; I am enough," he is shouting it loud and clear. There is a particular arrogance that sticks to a person who is spiritually bereft by his own choice. His lack of understanding makes him impossible to reason with and usually difficult to please.

Scott is this kind of fool. He is a pastor of a large church. He is charming and has a very charismatic personality that draws people to him. He prays beautiful prayers, visits the sick, and always shows up at the funeral home with a good word. That is his winsome side.

On the other hand, he is perfectionistic, petulant, and often prideful when he deals with his staff. If they don't do everything as he would do it, he gets mad. If he can't be in control, he becomes almost frenzied. His paranoia kicks in, and he becomes a bully until he can regain control. He truly is his own source and resource, although he preaches about trusting God for everything.

Hardened

The third word translated as fool is *ewil*, used nineteen times in Proverbs. This word seems to characterize the longstanding fool: the "dirty old man"; the nagging, whining "my way or no way" woman; people who have spurned God for so long and have detested knowledge for so many years that they have become crusty and unbendable. Proverbs 1:7 describes them well: "The fear of the LORD is the beginning of knowledge; but fools despise wisdom and discipline."

BUT MY FOOL ISN'T SO BAD!

After looking honestly at the characteristics of a fool, you might be thinking, *Well, I do see some of those negative qualities in my difficult person, and I've experienced some unpleasant consequences when I've come up against them. But my fool has a lot of good qualities too! Is it really fair to focus on everything that's wrong and minimize the fact that the person who causes me difficulty can be lovable as well?*

That's a good point, one that keeps so many of us hooked into relational dynamics that take a terrible toll. What you must watch out for is thinking a fool will have no appeal, will be obnoxious and always difficult, and that there is no way you could love him. In reality we love our fools, and that's what makes our relationships with them painful.

Recently when I was speaking about "Loving Our Fools" at a conference in the Northwest, I had shared the profile of a fool with all its negative characteristics, and I was about to address the issue that we love our fools not for their bad qualities but for the parts of them that are good, warm, and fun-loving. I casually turned to the audience and asked if anyone could think of a reason why an individual would love his or her fool. Almost before I got the words out of my mouth, one woman shouted out, "Christmas presents!" Her response brought down the house, but the reality was that many women in the audience knew what she was talking about. Her husband's Christmas presents were so great, she was willing to overlook his destructive foolishness in order to enjoy them!

The woman who owned up to the reason she loved her fool was like many women with whom I have spoken. When she shouted out her answer, my mind immediately went to another woman I had met several years ago. Claudia was married to a humdinger. He earned big money, made big decisions, and created big ordeals when he wasn't pleased. She had learned that if she just weathered the storm, he would reward her "faithfulness" in staying with him. She hated her own behavior because it felt so opportunistic, and in many ways she guessed it really was. She put up with Chuck, and Chuck put out for her!

In her most rational moments, Claudia hated the fear she saw on their children's faces when Chuck came home a little drunk and a lot abusive. When he screamed, she hurt for the pain she saw in her son Chap's face. Her daughter, Claire, worried her too. It was hard to see the girl so depressed when her dad upbraided her for some teenage misdemeanor. Claudia had learned to withdraw and keep a low profile, knowing that when Chuck's foolish rage was over he would be sorry and whatever she wanted she could have. Claudia liked her jewelry, her cars, and her shopping sprees. She loved the side of her fool that gave her gifts and "kept" her in the manner to which she definitely had become accustomed!

Many of the people I've talked with can easily describe the lovable side of their fool. They speak of creativity, charm, charisma, and intelligence. Julie qualifies in each of those areas. Her husband, James, vows those are the characteristics that drew him to her. He loved the way she thought. It was so "off the wall" it looked like life with her would be "the great adventure." Instead, life with Julie turned into a surreal experience where James was never quite sure what to expect or what was expected. Until her creative charm got her involved with another man, James loved that unpredictable side of his beloved fool, Julie.

Life with a fool, whoever it might be, can be so off balance that one day you see the negative, strident, unbending side, and the next you experience the benevolent, ingratiating, generous side. While your mind is processing what you are seeing and hearing, your heart is having to translate what you are feeling. The problem is that you are usually cycling through the whole experience fairly rapidly, and rarely do your mind and your heart fall into step with one another. No wonder you feel so crazy.

THE BENEFITS OF BREAKING FREE

Staying involved with a fool in an up-close and personal way may offer many perceived benefits: security, companionship, approval, social or financial success, a sense of identity, conflict avoidance. But when we are blinded by these "benefits," it's easy to overlook the enormous cost of maintaining the status quo.

Debbie spoke with dismay about her ignorance early in her relationship with Charlie. "I didn't know we were so sick until we were invited to visit other people's homes. They didn't seem to live in the chaos we did. They were able to make plans and stick to them. They were able to sit with one another and have a conversation. They could relax and just let things happen without always trying to decipher some hidden agenda. That was the beginning for me. I knew there had to be a better way to live."

And then there was Annie, who had walked on eggshells with Grace for years. They were neighbors who raised their children together. For the most part the women got along, but if Grace ever became angry over some supposed slight or perceived injustice, she punished Annie by pouting or sometimes refusing to talk. At one point in their relationship they went for eight months without speaking. Annie wrote notes, left voicemail messages, and tried to break down the barriers between herself and her friend. It was to no avail until Grace decided it was acceptable for them to communicate again.

During that time, Annie began to see what was happening and what a toll the relationship was taking on her. Although she was grateful that Grace had called a truce and decided to rekindle their relationship, she had experienced the freedom of not having to please Grace and bend over backward to earn her approval. From that day on, Annie was no longer willing to tiptoe around her friend and wait for Grace to be the sole definer of how the relationship would work. She chose instead to keep her distance, to breathe new air that Grace could not pollute. They continued to see one another occasionally, but the atmosphere was totally different. No longer was Annie controlled by Grace's tactics, and Grace knew it.

Foolproofing our lives isn't easy. Our fools are lovable…and cunning. Engaging…and threatening. Learning to relate to them without being sucked into their emotional undertow takes time and tenacity. But to a person, the people I have talked with who have successfully altered the "balance of power" in their most difficult relationships say things like, "I have a new identity, improved self-esteem, freedom to be an adult, the ability to hear God, and phenomenal spiritual vitality." No longer are they forced to revolve around the vortex of their fool. Finally they have an opportunity to discover who they really are apart from the swirling upheaval caused by their crazy-making relationship.

Dave and Renee experienced this liberation when they challenged the verbal negativity of Renee's father, Richard. Early in his marriage to Renee, Dave saw the power her dad had over her. Richard would frequently call and intimidate Renee with angry, strife-filled conversation, and each time she was devastated.

After many hours of talking, Dave and Renee determined that they would make a united stand against her dad's verbal onslaughts. Not one to see someone he loves tormented, Dave, with Renee's permission, confronted her dad the next time he called. In the kindest but firmest way possible, Dave said, "Richard, it is important that we work out a way to have a conversation without all the negative words that are destroying Renee. You are welcome to call or visit our home anytime, but that behavior toward her is unacceptable."

Not knowing what Richard would do, Dave and Renee put it all on the line. In many ways, they lost. Richard hung up cursing and promising that Dave had made a big mistake. The relationship was put on hold that day, and now, several years later there has been no reconnection. But in many ways, Dave and Renee won. They are united in their mutual commitment to peace in their home and peace with one another. Peace with Richard would be nice, but his choices have left Dave and Renee with no other options. This is a man who, because he is always right in his own mind and because he trusts in his own heart, cannot see that he has willingly lost a daughter—just so he can be "right"!

As we explore the way a fool thinks and acts in the chapters ahead, you may see that your entanglement with the difficult person in your life is costing you too much and doing your fool no good either. It's time to wise up. Believe me, please, when I tell you that you can't just wait and hope things will change. Like wishing a cancer away, waiting out a fool can be deadly.

My prayer for you is that you will be liberated from the chains that bind you and keep you believing, *If only I could act a certain way, this relationship would work.* I also pray you will be freed of the lie that says it doesn't matter what you do. There *is* a way to stop the pain. There *is* hope for peace of mind and healthy relating. You don't have to be controlled by the fool you love.

As you continue your journey through the pages ahead, I pray that God will reveal himself to you as a safe haven. As you seek his will and his heart, I believe you will find his wisdom for your situation.

If you have ever felt foolish, you may be hard-pressed to come to grips with the reality that you may be trying to relate to a bona fide fool. When faced with your own failures, it can be difficult to recognize the difference between making foolish choices and being foolish by character. But if you want to successfully foolproof your life, it is critical that you know what kind of folly you're dealing with in yourself and in others.

Think About It

Honestly answering the following questions could help you clarify the "flavor" of fool with which you may be dealing. This is not an exhaustive list of the different varieties of foolishness, but I hope it will give you food for thought.

1. Is your difficult person honest at least part of the time?

2. Will he eventually tell you the truth even if it doesn't make him look good?

3. Does he repeat the same acts over and over?

4. Does it appear that he tries to change?

5. Does it appear that your fool learns for a while and then "forgets" what he has learned?

6. Does your fool win you over by charming you?

7. Does your fool "win" by intimidation?

8. Does your fool reject all counsel, whether through a counselor, a tape, a book, or a radio or television program?

9. Is he easily angered? Is the problem always your fault?

10. Do you see any reverence for God in your fool?

If you answered questions 1-6 mostly with yes and 7-10 mostly with no, then more than likely you are dealing with a simple or naive person. If you answered questions 7-10 mostly with yes and 1-6 mostly with no, then you are probably dealing with a bona fide fool.

11. If you think you are dealing with a naive or simple person, jot down your personal experience with his behavior.

12. If you think you are dealing with a hard-core fool, describe his behavior.

13. If you aren't sure what variety of fool you're dealing with, note why you are unsure.

Go to God About It

1. As you turn to God for comfort and understanding, think about what he says to those who are open to him and who embrace his ways. Read the following scriptures. Then, in the space below, make notes about what his Word says you will glean if you choose to reverence him.

Psalm 111:10

The fear of the LORD is the beginning of wisdom;
    all who follow his precepts have good understanding.
To him belongs eternal praise.

Psalm 37:23-24

If the LORD delights in a man's way,
    he makes his steps firm;
though he stumble, he will not fall,
    for the LORD upholds him with his hand.

Psalm 92:12-15

The righteous will flourish like a palm tree,
    they will grow like a cedar of Lebanon;
planted in the house of the LORD,
    they will flourish in the courts of our God.
They will still bear fruit in old age,
    they will stay fresh and green,

proclaiming, "The LORD is upright;

he is my Rock, and there is no wickedness in him."

2. What does God want from you? Make note of it in the margin.

Psalm 51:15-17

O Lord, open my lips,

and my mouth will declare your praise.

You do not delight in sacrifice, or I would bring it;

you do not take pleasure in burnt offerings.

The sacrifices of God are a broken spirit;

a broken and contrite heart,

O God, you will not despise.

Consult the Bible About It

1. Read these words and note what you discover about simple or naive people. What are the characteristics that seem significant to you? Make a list of the words used in the following verses that describe the simple or naive person.

Proverbs 9:13-18

The woman Folly is loud;

she is undisciplined and without knowledge.

She sits at the door of her house,

on a seat at the highest point of the city,

calling out to those who pass by,

who go straight on their way.

"Let all who are simple come in here!"
    she says to those who lack judgment.
"Stolen water is sweet;
    food eaten in secret is delicious!"
But little do they know that the dead are there,
    that her guests are in the depths of the grave.

Proverbs 21:11

When a mocker is punished, the simple gain wisdom;
    when a wise man is instructed, he gets knowledge.

Proverbs 22:3

A prudent man sees danger and takes refuge,
    but the simple keep going and suffer for it.

2. Note the warning God gives to the simple, the mocker, and the fool.

Proverbs 1:22-27

How long will you simple ones love your simple ways?
    How long will mockers delight in mockery
    and fools hate knowledge?
If you had responded to my rebuke,
    I would have poured out my heart to you
    and made my thoughts known to you.
But since you rejected me when I called
    and no one gave heed when I stretched out my hand,
since you ignored all my advice
    and would not accept my rebuke,
I in turn will laugh at your disaster;

I will mock when calamity overtakes you—
when calamity overtakes you like a storm,
    when disaster sweeps over you like a whirlwind,
    when distress and trouble overwhelm you.

3. Make notes in the margin concerning any hope the simple or naive person might have.

Proverbs 1:32-33
For the waywardness of the simple will kill them,
    and the complacency of fools will destroy them;
but whoever listens to me will live in safety
    and be at ease, without fear of harm.

4. Summarize in your own words what the Word of God—which includes his law, his statutes, his precepts, his commands, and his ordinances—offers to the simple. What does the Word offer to the servant of the Lord?

Psalm 19:7-11
The law of the LORD is perfect,
    reviving the soul.
The statutes of the LORD are trustworthy,
    making wise the simple.
The precepts of the LORD are right,
    giving joy to the heart.
The commands of the LORD are radiant,
    giving light to the eyes.
The fear of the LORD is pure,
    enduring forever.

The ordinances of the LORD are sure
    and altogether righteous.
They are more precious than gold,
    than much pure gold;
they are sweeter than honey,
    than honey from the comb.
By them is your servant warned;
    in keeping them there is great reward.

Psalm 119:130
The unfolding of your words gives light;
    it gives understanding to the simple.

5. Specifically, what will wisdom do for the simple?

Proverbs 9:1-6
Wisdom has built her house;
    she has hewn out its seven pillars.
She has prepared her meat and mixed her wine;
    she has also set her table.
She has sent out her maids, and she calls
    from the highest point of the city.
"Let all who are simple come in here!"
    she says to those who lack judgment.
"Come, eat my food
    and drink the wine I have mixed.
Leave your simple ways and you will live;
    walk in the way of understanding."

Proverbs 9:10-12

The fear of the LORD is the beginning of wisdom,

and knowledge of the Holy One is understanding.

For through me your days will be many,

and years will be added to your life.

If you are wise, your wisdom will reward you;

if you are a mocker, you alone will suffer.

6. Now we turn to a different flavor of fool. Note in the margin what the following scriptures tell you about this kind of fool.

Psalm 94:8

Take heed, you senseless ones among the people;

you fools, when will you become wise?

Psalm 92:5-7

How great are your works, O LORD,

how profound your thoughts!

The senseless man does not know,

fools do not understand,

that though the wicked spring up like grass

and all evildoers flourish,

they will be forever destroyed.

Psalm 74:22

Rise up, O God, and defend your cause;

remember how fools mock you all day long.

7. Do you see any hope in the following scriptures for a hard-core fool? If so, what is it?

Psalm 107:17-20

Some became fools through their rebellious ways

and suffered affliction because of their iniquities.

They loathed all food

and drew near the gates of death.

Then they cried to the LORD in their trouble,

and he saved them from their distress.

He sent forth his word and healed them;

he rescued them from the grave.

What Will You Do About It?

1. Memorize the following verse and cling to it in the weeks ahead. You will need to embrace this truth to be able to deal with your fool wisely.

   Proverbs 9:10

   The fear of the LORD is the beginning of wisdom,

   and knowledge of the Holy One is understanding.

2. Return to the prayer you pasted on the flyleaf of this book. Pray in your own words, asking God to do what only he can do in your life first and then in the life of your fool.

As he thinks within himself, so he is.

PROVERBS 23:7, NASB

We do not live to think, but, on the contrary,
we think in order that we may succeed in surviving.

JOSÉ ORTEGA Y GASSET

Either you think—or else others have to think for you
and take power from you, pervert and discipline your natural tastes,
civilize and sterilize you.

F. SCOTT FITZGERALD

To think is to act.

RALPH WALDO EMERSON

CHAPTER THREE

"If He Thinks Like a Fool..."

If you want to be successful in foolproofing your life, you must know how a fool thinks. Character—good or bad—is developed as a mind is developed. The way we think determines what we do, how we do it, and whether we have any motivation to change. A fool is not created overnight. The bent of his mind is developed over years of responding to life in a certain way.

A fool has a distinctive, consistent way of thinking. If you pay attention, you will begin to notice a rather simple grid through which your fool processes life experiences. You will also be able to figure out why your fool does what he does. This insight will in turn help you realize how your own thinking needs to change around your difficult relationship. I have been fascinated to discover that there are several indicators—"red flags," if you will—that pop up when you encounter a person who qualifies as a fool. Every fool thinks the same way when it comes to some basics.

A FOOL IS ALWAYS "RIGHT"

Self-reliant and self-centered, a fool rejects all attempts to reason with him. As mentioned in the last chapter, he believes that his thoughts are true and his actions are acceptable because they are his. "The way of a fool is right in his own eyes, but a wise man is he who listens to counsel" (Proverbs 12:15, NASB). That's simple enough. Look for a person who will listen to feedback and advice, and you will more than likely find someone who wants to be wise. If, on the other hand, you see someone who balks at seeking counsel and refuses to accept feedback, you may have a fool on your hands. It certainly is a red flag, no matter what.

Beth saw this red flag when she met Bob. He was an outstanding athlete and the kind of student who seemed able to tackle and subdue any subject he encountered. He had a great personality, but he just couldn't tolerate disagreement from anyone. He was a sharp guy, so he was usually right. Even Beth thought that, but the longer she was around him the more she saw this side of him that was so unbendable.

Believing that Bob would become more open to influence and give-and-take if they were married, Beth foolishly joined her life with his. Bob was in his residency as a surgeon, and Beth held on to her belief that Bob's problem with "always being right" would diminish once he was in his own practice. Sadly, she found that if anyone was going to get better, it would have to be her. Bob was totally closed to any discussion that would even hint that he had a problem. When things were good, they were good. Bob was gracious, kind to Beth, and full of fun. It was only when a difficulty arose that he was "right" no matter what. There was one opinion in their household, and it was his! Beth suggested counseling when they hit a particularly sensitive issue between them. Bob refused, and that was that.

More times than I care to recall I have met with people (usually women but not always) who have said, "I begged my mate to come with me to get some help, but he refused." The usual rebuff was, "Why would I want to do that?" As if there is nothing that possibly could be wrong with him, the fool staunchly refuses the counsel of anyone who might have a different perspective than his. That's why we categorize this kind of person as a fool: "The fear of the LORD is the beginning of knowledge, but fools despise wisdom and discipline" (Proverbs 1:7).

A FOOL IS SELF-CONTAINED

Not only are fools' ways right in their own eyes, but they also trust in themselves alone. There is a certain sad, lonely air about a fool, even when he is most cocky. Proverbs 28:26 says, "He who trusts in his own heart is a fool, but he who walks wisely will be delivered" (NASB). The words literally mean that fools have confidence in and put their total reliance on their own "inner selves." Fools believe that they know whatever they need to know because they have learned to put their unqualified trust in their own resources.

Tom Barton is that kind of man. He was ten when his dad left home. Tommy had mixed feelings about it all. His daddy had played ball with him sometimes, but just as often he had sat in the den, channel surfing. There had been nights when Tommy had heard his mother raising her voice, but he had never heard his dad say anything. Then one Saturday, his dad packed his bags and left. His mother locked herself in her bedroom and cried. Tommy sat on the back steps watching a bee buzz in a lilac bush and wondered what would happen next.

Tommy grew up to become "Tom," but he continually felt like "little Tommy," forever wondering what was going to happen. This one fact profoundly affected how he related to people. He trusted no one and became a loner. He liked to be around the guys sometimes, but he often felt profound mistrust. He didn't have to have a reason. He just became uncomfortable, felt insecure, and withdrew.

As a teenager, Tom determined that he was the safest when the walls he had built around himself were the highest. His mother wanted him to be involved in all the activities that young people in his town were into, and his teachers encouraged him as well. On one or two occasions, he ventured into areas that others thought he would be good in, but he was just too uncomfortable. He felt so out of control.

His mother was concerned about him, so she sent him to a church youth group and asked John, the youth minister, to look out after her Tommy. No matter what John said or did, however, Tom stayed isolated and self-contained. He didn't need or want what John had to offer. He was doing all right. His thinking was frozen in a self-protective pattern that could not tolerate questions or input from outside sources. He trusted only in what he believed, in what felt safe. Unfortunately, he was on the sad path toward developing the mind-set of a fool, a mind-set that insists, "The rest of the world is really skewed, but I am okay."

This chronic way of thinking is developed when people, out of their own neediness, try to become their own need-meeters. Such a position is not uncommon; we all try it. The difference between fools and wise persons is that when wise people discover they can't meet their own needs, eventually they look somewhere else.

I remember almost the very moment in my own life when it occurred to me that I could not meet all my own needs. I was an idealistic twenty-five-year-old. I had all the relationships I wanted, I lived where I wanted to live, and I didn't appear to have anything to worry about…but deep inside I was empty. I realized there was something far greater going on in this world than me and my concerns and that I needed to open my mind to understand what life was about. The thought hit me like a bolt out of the blue: *It's not about you, Jan.* My slow discovery of truth began as I searched out the mystery of a God who was sovereign and who ultimately controlled the world. I had a need, and I desperately desired a need-meeter. It was at that point that I gave all I knew of me to all I knew of God. I wasn't sure what that meant, but I knew I needed someone outside myself to give my life direction and substance.

For every person, this is the moment of transformation. *I cannot be confident in myself. I need more. I require a need-meeter, and I am willing to humbly acknowledge it.* Fools never get to this desperate point; they never make inquiry of anyone outside themselves. Even those who maintain all the trappings of religiosity can be fools in pious disguise. Fools stubbornly maintain their position at all costs. Once they believe an idea is right, it is set in cement. They are unmoved by new ideas that challenge their perspective. That is not to say they won't ever embrace a new thought or concept if they are convinced that it's to their advantage.

Remember, the thinking of a fool does not necessarily encompass his whole world. The fool may be a very innovative thinker in his profession. Fools may shrewdly see the wisdom of good investments, or they may seize an opportunity to make an advantageous move for their personal advancement. Generally, however, they refuse to embrace any thought that might invade their comfort zone. They steadfastly maintain that they are "enough," and if they find that not to be true, they will create the situations or find the people who can do for them what they need to have done.

Unlike the naive or simple soul who "falls" into foolish thinking and behavior, Tom holds to his perspective like a dog on a bone. He is determined to stick with it at all costs—to himself or to anyone he might try to have a relationship with.

Tom's wife, Carla, saw the hurting little boy in Tom and not so wisely believed she could kiss his hurts away. Marriage would be the answer for the pain of his life. Now both of them are struggling. Tom likes the way Carla makes him feel, but he has a difficult time accepting her need for any life apart from their cloistered realm. Carla is a people person, and yet her life is so entangled with Tom's that she has sublimated her personality in order to confine herself to his small, safe world. Carla's hope that her loving attention would empower Tom to break out of his self-protective bubble has been dashed. Tom's insecurity has only surfaced more and more, and in an attempt to keep Carla where he wants her, Tom has tightened his defenses around their relationship. He has become more rigidly demanding of her time and cynically derogatory of her feeble attempts to be involved with other people. They have gotten to the point of separation on more than one occasion, but then with tears and promises Tom loosens his grip, Carla acquiesces, and the crazy cycle begins again.

Unfortunately, this is one of the hurtful effects of loving your distrustful, insulated fool. Like an insect who approaches a Venus flytrap, the one who believes real relationship is possible doesn't see the danger until it's too late. Then the walls snap shut, and unless an escape route can be found, the result is death to hopes, dreams, and intimacy.

A FOOL IS DECEITFUL

As I've already mentioned, there are two sides to every fool. The appealing, needy, sometimes even "godly"-looking side invites you in, but the trap is set. Proverbs 14:8 warns us that "the folly of fools is deception." Fools hide their true natures until they can get what they want. They have learned over the years to hide who they really are, but they venture out of their self-protective world just far enough to dangle the hook—and usually they "catch" compassionate people who think they can "help."

Once the "fish" is hooked, the fool is in total control, and a perverted form of intimacy is accomplished. I say "perverted" because it is a closeness based on living a lie. Healthy intimacy thrives only when two people are able and willing to be honest with each other and allow each other to be who they really are. Fools are much too frightened to risk this kind of intimacy, so they lure their "fish" with the appearance of closeness. Such false intimacy, based on neediness and control, eventually kills the fish.

If this illustration is a bit "back to nature" for you, perhaps you'll relate more to Bryan, who learned the hard way that what you see is not always what you've been told you will get! Bryan was the kind of guy who would be any mother's dream catch for her daughter—sensitive, easygoing, hardworking, thoughtful. He was such a great guy it was hard for his family and friends to believe he had married Jean.

He met her while working in another state, and they were engaged before his family even met her. When Bryan brought Jean home to announce their engagement, there was something that just didn't sit well with Bryan's mom and sisters. Jean had an edge when she spoke to Bryan that made them uneasy. They didn't speak of it between themselves until several months later when there was a return visit. This time, Jean's "edge" was full-blown. She sat in the den reading while the rest of the family prepared dinner and eventually ate together. She left the room when anyone came in and tried to talk with her. She retreated to the bedroom early in the evening and often didn't emerge until lunchtime. The first two days Bryan made excuses, but when his sister Tam cornered him with a pointed question about Jean's behavior, tears filled his eyes as he said, "Tam, I can't explain it. She has become the wife from hell!"

Bryan admitted to his sister that he had married Jean without knowing her well. She had been married before but told him that her husband had been abusive. Bryan thought it unnecessary to inquire any further because she seemed so totally right for him. They dated for several months, went to church together, prayed, and even studied the Bible together. Soon after the marriage, however, the "real" Jean began to emerge as a domineering shrew who raged and laughed at Bryan if she didn't get her way. Bewildered, he made the inquiries he should have made before he and Jean approached the altar. He discovered the profile of an individual he wouldn't have recognized as Jean, except now he had lived with her for several months and knew he'd uncovered the truth.

How could he have been so wrong? How could he have missed the side of Jean that was so destructive? He hadn't seen the red flag of deception. Jean presented her "good" side to get what she wanted. While she gave plenty of clues to the truth while they were dating, it wasn't until she removed her mask and allowed her true character to be exposed that Bryan saw the devastating mistake he had made.

A FOOL IS COMPLACENT

When those who think like fools have established themselves within their self-protective environment, they are at rest. Proverbs contains a short statement that describes this state: "For the waywardness of the naive shall kill them, and the complacency of fools shall destroy them" (1:32, NASB). Complacency, in this context, implies restfulness, peacefulness, satisfaction. Even a fool's own sin doesn't bother him. Since fools are their own judge and jury, they are confident in declaring themselves innocent. They are perfectly content with themselves. They are who they are.

We all know one or two people like Ella. She is a complacent old lady who has used her rapier tongue and sarcastic words to communicate her will and ways to those she calls near and dear. Her own grandchildren avoid her. One even asked his dad, "Is Granny Ella the antichrist?"

Through the years, Ella's sisters have talked with her about her tongue. Her long- suffering husband tried to reason with her. Even her two daughters, whom she brags about behind their backs, asked her to think about what her words were doing to their children. But with her usual bravado Ella replied, "I'm not hurting those kids. I don't say anything they haven't heard on TV. You two are just a couple of bleeding hearts. You never have had any starch in your backbones!"

Proverbs 14:9 says, "Fools mock at making amends for sin." Trying to get Ella to change is an impossible task because she is complacent about her sin. She is unmoved by the appeals of those she claims to love. She is insulated in her own world and has no intention of letting anyone rock her boat. When anyone dares to mention that she might need to curb her tongue, she acts hurt. The tears come, "you don't understand" gushes forth, and the person who has dared to confront her feels confused and guilty. Everyone feels bad, except Ella! She is satisfied.

If you have such a person in your life, then you know how it is. It's the wildest thing: You know you are right, and you believe you should say something. But the minute you do, it all gets turned around, and somehow you have become the troublemaker.

At its core, foolish thinking is always selfish. The fool has to protect his own interests at all costs. Proverbs 14:16 says, "A wise man is cautious and turns away from evil, but a fool is arrogant and careless" (NASB). The Hebrew word for *arrogant* describes someone who "crosses over all boundaries"; the word *careless* indicates a person is "overly self-confident." He is right and will do whatever it takes to get what he wants. The fool determines to accept no challenge to his thinking. To do so would rock his whole world. Each rejection of counsel and each negation of instruction carves the fool's character. The fool's mind is set, and everyone in his world must revolve around him. The fool's self-satisfaction keeps him on a steady, though destructive, course. Although trying to relate to the fool is crazy-making for you, the fool is okay in his own mind.

Once you understand the mind-set of the fool in your life, you can alter your approach accordingly. We will talk more about what you can do differently in the last section of this book. Until we get there, let's keep looking at what you can expect from the foolish, difficult person who's taken up residence in your life.

The way a person thinks is at the very core of all that he is. The way you think drives who you are, just as the way the fool thinks drives who he is. Unfortunately, because the fool is characterized by self-reliance and self-containment, his thinking goes unchallenged. As a result, the fool seals himself in a bubble that becomes impenetrable.

Think About It

1. What kind of thinking characterizes your fool?

2. How do you see this thinking affecting your fool's behavior?

3. How does your fool's behavior affect you? (In other words, how is your behavior influenced by him?)

4. What do you think about that? Are you pleased with your behavior, or are you displeased? Why?

Go to God About It

As you meditate on the following "snapshots" from Scripture, sum up what you see about your thoughts. Note your observations in the margin.

Psalm 139:2-4

You know when I sit and when I rise;
>   you perceive my thoughts from afar.
You discern my going out and my lying down;
>   you are familiar with all my ways.
Before a word is on my tongue
>   you know it completely, O LORD.

Proverbs 15:26

The LORD detests the thoughts of the wicked,
>   but those of the pure are pleasing to him.

Isaiah 55:7

Let the wicked forsake his way
>   and the evil man his thoughts.
Let him turn to the LORD, and he will have mercy on him,
>   and to our God, for he will freely pardon.

Matthew 9:4

Knowing their thoughts, Jesus said, "Why do you entertain evil thoughts in your hearts?"

Matthew 15:19-20

For out of the heart come evil thoughts, murder, adultery, sexual immorality, theft, false testimony, slander. These are what make a man "unclean"; but eating with unwashed hands does not make him "unclean."

Deuteronomy 29:16-19

You yourselves know how we lived in Egypt and how we passed through the countries on the way here. You saw among them their detestable images and idols of wood and stone, of silver and gold. Make sure there is no man or woman, clan or tribe among you today whose heart turns away from the Lord our God to go and worship the gods of those nations; make sure there is no root among you that produces such bitter poison.

When such a person hears the words of this oath, he invokes a blessing on himself and therefore thinks, "I will be safe, even though I persist in going my own way." This will bring disaster on the watered land as well as the dry.

Galatians 6:3

If anyone thinks he is something when he is nothing, he deceives himself.

Jeremiah 4:14

O Jerusalem, wash the evil from your heart and be saved.

How long will you harbor wicked thoughts?

Can you see how significant "thinking" can be?

Consult the Bible About It

1. The Lord has a lot to say about his own thoughts. Read the following passage and mark everything he says about his thoughts.

> ### Isaiah 55:7-9
>
> Let the wicked forsake his way
> > and the evil man his thoughts.
>
> Let him turn to the LORD, and he will have mercy on him,
> > and to our God, for he will freely pardon.
>
> "For my thoughts are not your thoughts,
> > neither are your ways my ways,"
> > > declares the LORD.
>
> "As the heavens are higher than the earth,
> > so are my ways higher than your ways
> > and my thoughts than your thoughts."

2. Note in the margin what a person must do to correct his thoughts.

3. From your observations at this time, would your fool consider changing his thoughts? How do you know?

What Will You Do About It?

1. From your own examination of yourself, will you change your thoughts? Why or why not?

2. List some thoughts you have held that you are considering changing.

3. Can you see how 2 Corinthians 10:5 is a tool you could use to align your thoughts with God's thoughts? If so, how?

   2 Corinthians 10:5
   We demolish arguments and every pretension that sets itself up against the knowledge of God, and we take captive every thought to make it obedient to Christ.

4. In your own words, write out a brief prayer telling the Lord what you want your thoughts to look like and the greatest struggle you have with them. Admit you are powerless to change the thinking of your fool, but assume responsibility for what you do with your own thoughts, and ask God to make them pure and wise.

Guard your steps when you go to the house of God.
Go near to listen rather than to offer the sacrifice of fools,
who do not know that they do wrong.

ECCLESIASTES 5:1

A fool's paradise is a wise man's hell!

THOMAS FULLER

Destiny: a tyrant's authority for crime
and a fool's excuse for failure.

AMBROSE BIERCE

However big the fool,
there is always a bigger fool to admire him.

NICOLAS BOILEAU-DESPRÉAUX

CHAPTER FOUR

Foolish Is As Foolish Does

"Be careful! You're only going to make her mad!" Linda had heard those words from her dad ever since she could remember. He had retreated to a "just be careful" mode early in his marriage to Linda's mother. When he discovered that things were going to be her way or no way and that to cross her was far more traumatic than just letting her be, he withdrew into an emotional corner. He tried to warn Linda and her brother, Evan, but being children, they tested the limits and proved him to be right. They only made their mother mad!

Linda was in her midtwenties when she began to realize that both her parents were angry people. Her mother was the one who was quick to speak her mind. It didn't matter what the subject was, if it wasn't in line with her way of thinking, there was a fight. There was no doubt how her mother felt about things, and it was evident there wasn't much that pleased her.

Linda's dad, on the other hand, was mild-mannered by comparison. He wasn't volatile like her mom, but he was a master of the little jab. With sarcastic comments and passive-aggressive responses, he retaliated toward Linda's mom on a daily basis. The tension in the household was ever present. Linda often felt that if her mother wasn't upset over something or if her dad fell silent and wasn't picking at her mother, the house was dead. There just wasn't anything else to her parents' relationship.

As an adult, Linda realized how profoundly she had been influenced by her parents' behavior. She hated what she heard coming out of her own mouth and what she felt as her first response to anything that didn't please her. She usually recognized the effect as she saw people around her withering. She determined to bring the insanity to a halt. Assuming responsibility for change was harder than she had imagined because the behavior was so ingrained, but Linda was determined to break out of her old patterns. At times, she felt like the pictures she had seen of weak little birds pecking away at their shells in order to break free and be born. It was that traumatic and life-changing for her, but today she would tell you it was well worth all of the effort. She has to keep her guard up because her parents' ways can still be second nature sometimes, but she has learned she doesn't have to live as the clone of her angry parents.

The person who is foolish by character could not imagine going through the kind of process Linda did. He would be exhausted...but more than that, he would look weak and vulnerable, and that just wouldn't be acceptable! Because he sees nothing wrong with what he says, never observes the impact of his words on others, and assumes no responsibility for change, he wouldn't consider questioning himself. It would be too disruptive.

Just as a fool's thinking runs in some predictable grooves, so his behavior has some distinctives you'd be wise to recognize.

A FOOL IS ANGRY

"A fool finds no pleasure in understanding but delights in airing his own opinions" (Proverbs 18:2). You probably know people like this and can even put a face with this description. This is the immediately recognizable individual who blusters and draws attention to herself. She tells you what she thinks and doesn't wait for a rebuttal. As far as she is concerned, there is no rebuttal that will stand. She is right, and if you don't believe her, just ask her! Of course, daring to say you have doubts will usually get you in trouble, so it often feels better just to let the issue pass uncontested. A person who can bear no challenge and who lets you know it by her behavior is an angry individual.

There is another type of fool, however, that we often are hasty to overlook: the soft-spoken charmer who is fine until pressure comes to bear. Then this person is quick-tempered, sullen, or contemptuous. Whether the anger is expressed in an icy silence, a furious outburst, or a mocking verbal slap, you have no doubt you have incurred his displeasure.

Have you ever tried to have a conversation with your difficult person and had him laugh at you? Have you ever said something in the most sincere way you knew and found your thoughts were totally discounted? A key passage in Proverbs describes this kind of behavior: "When a wise man has a controversy with a foolish man, the foolish man either rages or laughs, and there is no rest" (Proverbs 29:9, NASB). The raging or laughing throws you off balance, and "no rest" is the result.

When you experience the blistering fire, dry ice, or mincing scorn of someone's anger on a fairly consistent basis, you have a strong clue that you are dealing with a fool. The fool uses anger the way a person with a black belt in karate uses his feet. *Swish! Wham!* And you're on the mat before you know it, not sure what hit you! Since a fool's anger-based behavior takes many forms, it is easy to be thrown off guard.

Horace is the type of angry individual who would never let you know how he felt in person, but watch out for his letters! When he was with his sons and daughters, he would act as if everything was all right, but then they would receive one of his ripping letters that reeked of manipulation and self-service. He seemed to target his daughter, Mary Ellen, with his most pointed attacks. He would treat her with gentleness and seeming respect—until she tried to become her own person. Then he would attack with fury, pointing out her shortcomings and her lack of appreciation for what she had received from him as her loving father. The fat envelope with his handwritten tome made her hands shake and gave her dry mouth whenever she discovered one in her mailbox. It always came without warning. She may have just enjoyed a pleasant visit to her parents' house only to discover her father's scorching document waiting for her when she returned home.

The other children received similar letters, but unlike Mary Ellen, they discarded them before they read them. Mary Ellen fell for it every time. She could not give up the hope that "this time he's going to say something kind." Disappointed, she would often sink into despair because she found it so hard to accept that her father, who could be so good to her, would turn so quickly to point out the things he saw as weaknesses in her. The way he expressed himself left her feeling beaten and defenseless.

A FOOL CREATES STRIFE

Quarrels, confusion, chaos, and strife seem to swirl around a fool like dirt hovers around the character Pigpen in the Peanuts cartoon series. If Pigpen is anywhere around, a little floating pile of dust surrounds him. That's the way it is with a fool's behavior. A perfectly calm event can be turned into a fiasco when your beloved fool blows into the setting.

Now remember, creating disorder isn't necessarily what the fool's behavior is intended to do. He doesn't arrive on the scene planning to create a problem. But because his mind-set revolves around himself and because he is first and foremost self-protective, that's what happens. He doesn't see anyone else or how that person might be affected. If something happens, it is all about the fool—and others will somehow be blamed!

I was a guest on a radio call-in program when the topic was "Dealing with the Holidays." The holidays never fail to provide an environment where foolish behavior is showcased! One of the callers I talked with was concerned about her mother's Christmas visit. "For the first time in thirteen years," she said, "everyone will be here for Christmas. We're looking forward to it except for what probably is going to happen with my mother. When she visits, she comes through the door complaining. It's too hot or too cold. The food is served too late or too early. She doesn't like the squash recipe I use; she has a much better one. Honestly, by the time we're an hour into her visit, we are all at odds with one another. I'm really anxious about how it will be with my husband's family here too!" Experience had taught this caller that confusion and strife were coming in the door with her mother.

Again we can turn to the book of Proverbs and see that God has clearly spelled out what we can expect from a fool: "A fool's lips bring him strife, and his mouth invites a beating. A fool's mouth is his undoing, and his lips are a snare to his soul" (Proverbs 18:6-7). Isn't it interesting that the problems created by the fool usually seem to be associated with his mouth? The anger and deceit that fill the fool's heart bubble up into his mouth and spew out, creating strife and unrest.

Don't forget, however, that the fool has a beautiful side. A fool's behavior is consistently foolish in some areas, but often he is a multifaceted person who has the capacity to be charming in other areas. That is part of the chaotic nature of the interaction that throws you into

nfusion even though you see the foolish behavior with
d hear the schizophrenic talk with your own ears. It can
determine what is real.

A FOOL CAUSES DESTRUCTION

If you're significantly involved with a foolish person, you have probably
spent a good deal of time trying to find a way to get along with or to fix
him. Being consumed with your fool's behavior blinds you to what is
happening to *you*. Oh, you know you feel stuck and you're unhappy, and
if you're really honest, you know you've become what you never wanted
to be—angry, nagging, worried, or just plain discouraged. The sad truth
is that you may be all those things and still not see why you are where
you are.

I have seen many wonderful people who have staked their claim on
the lie that they could make a difference in the life of a fool by sacrific-
ing themselves. I have talked with parents who have given it all up to
salvage their child only to lose him in the end. I have seen adult children
stand at the coffin of a parent still hoping to feel approval that will never
come. I have seen husbands and wives willing to wait and wait while
their fool runs amuck—never calling time-out or insisting on an
encounter with the truth.

If there were any virtue in that course of action, I would say, "Take
it, and God bless you." But Scripture says, "He who walks with the wise
grows wise, but a companion of fools suffers harm" (Proverbs 13:20). It
is interesting to note that the word for *companion* in that verse means "a
special friend," or one who "grazes in the same pasture." The word for
fools is our classic definition "those who are stubborn, dull, arrogant."

And the word for *harm* means "destroyed." There is a sad inevitability
that you will suffer damage if you continue to relate closely with a fool.

Tim found this out when he tried to stay close to his mother, Bertha, and to protect her from his siblings' truthful accusations. Over many years, Bertha had proven herself to be a very manipulative woman.

When her daughters brought a halt to the insanity by backing away from close interaction with Bertha, Tim rose to his mom's defense with strong upbraiding of his sisters. "How could you treat her this way? She *is* your mother," he reminded them during every conversation.

But as Tim stayed close to Bertha, he paid a higher and higher price. She didn't appreciate anything he did for her. She verbally lashed him and talked about him to the rest of her family. "Tim, my worthless son, is hanging around me just asking for money." He felt compelled to try to make Bertha happy, but in the process he kept finding himself the butt of her derisive comments and slanderous statements.

The way Bertha exposed her foolishness to her son and inevitably to everyone she knew was through slander. No one's reputation or self-worth was safe with her. She just never "got it" that she had the power of life and death in her tongue. Inevitably, she chose death, death to everyone around her.

A FOOL SPREADS SLANDER

Assaulting the reputation and personal integrity of others is one more pattern for a fool. Proverbs 10:18 says, "He who conceals his hatred has lying lips, and whoever spreads slander is a fool."

Jo Ann was such a fool. A senior at a Christian college, Jo Ann had befriended Glenna, a freshman, and enjoyed the power she seemed to wield in her life. Glenna was a gentle-spirited, quiet girl who appreciated Jo Ann's attention. When Michaela arrived at midterm, she was assigned as a roommate to Glenna, and they quickly became close companions. Where Glenna was reserved, Michaela was outgoing. Where Glenna was pensive, Michaela was spontaneous. They truly enjoyed one another and seemed to blossom in one another's presence.

It took only a few weeks for Jo Ann to see that she had lost her control over Glenna. She still spent time with the freshman, but Glenna just wasn't as enamored with Jo Ann's attention or as easily swayed by her influence. It didn't take long for Glenna's new friend, Michaela, to become the target of Jo Ann's anger. She began to drop hints about Michaela and the things she had supposedly seen her doing. A slanderous word here, an innuendo there, and soon Michaela noticed that people were staying away from her.

When she was called into the dean's office and confronted with the fact that she had been accused of improper sexual behavior, she was devastated; and when she was told that this behavior was suspected to have occurred with Glenna, Michaela was shattered. Why would anyone say that about her? How could she possibly recover her reputation? The slander of a fool had taken a heavy toll on this free-spirited, loving girl.

A FOOL IS WEARISOME

There are times when the unrelenting foolishness of a fool can bring a sigh of, "Oh, please" from the one he is trying to con and a sardonic smile to anyone looking on. George and June's relationship presents a sad picture of the wearisome nature of a fool's wiles.

George had been involved in multiple affairs. His pattern was to be caught, to say he was sorry, to wine and dine his way back into the good graces of his wife, June, and then as soon as the dust settled to find another paramour for his pleasure. The last time it happened, instead of saying he was sorry and vowing never to seek the company of another woman again, George asked June just to be patient while he went out with Desirée one more time to tell her the affair was over.

The crazy part of this story is that he kept going out with Desirée time after time, telling June he had "just a few more things" he had to get straightened out with Desirée so they could make a clean break. With a straight face and deep sincerity in his blue eyes, he tried to convince June that she had a problem if she couldn't trust him! Finally, long-suffering June wised up and filed for divorce while George was "getting things straightened out" with Desirée.

Maybe you read this little scenario with a sad heart. Perhaps you haven't gone far enough in your journey to see anything to smile about. If you're entangled with a fool right now, I understand. You probably feel more like a small animal caught under a big rock. Proverbs 27:3 describes it like this: "Stone is heavy and sand a burden, but provocation by a fool is heavier than both." One of the maddening results of your fool's aggravation is the backwash that always seems to flow in your direction, splattering you with a stain of pain and disbelief. Just about the time you're congratulating yourself on emerging from the latest battle, your fool takes up arms again, and you're soon exhausted.

Hannah's sister, Jill, is the fool in her life. Just when Hannah thinks she has helped her find a place of safety and comfort, Jill will call about some scrape she's gotten herself into. Hannah loves her sister, but the provocation Jill creates leaves Hannah totally wiped out. Like Hannah, you may feel like you will never be disentangled. I hear you. That response is as consistent as the behavior of a fool. Fumes of hopelessness waft through the life of anyone who deals with a fool in a significant way.

A FOOL ENJOYS HIS FOOLISHNESS

One of the factors that makes involvement with a fool so stressful and wearisome is the fool's apparent delight in doing foolish things. A fool is like a teenager joyriding at high speeds just for the thrill of it while never noticing the danger he's causing himself and everyone around him. Proverbs 10:23 says, "A fool finds pleasure in evil conduct, but a man of understanding delights in wisdom." You and your beloved fool have two different aims. Even when he can manage to convince you with words that he is "right," you can see by his behavior that your goals are different.

Janelle's beloved fool is her younger brother, Sam, who stays in trouble with his unethical practices as a psychiatrist. He once had a brilliant future but threw it away through his evil, self-centered folly. In trouble with patients, with colleagues, and with medical boards in three states, Sam just laughs and moves every time the pressure is on.

Janelle is a model of responsibility. She cannot comprehend Sam's choices. He was raised in the same home, with the same good parents, and with ample opportunities to succeed; but his delight in conduct that is borderline criminal leaves her reeling. She is hopelessly impotent in the face of Sam's choices. She loves him but doesn't recognize the person he has become. When she mentions her deep concern for him, he hugs her, winks, and blows off her words with, "Oh, sis, don't worry about me. I'm too mean for anyone to bother." The fact that he is under indictment for fraudulent medical practices doesn't bother him at all.

THERE IS HOPE!

What you've read so far may be a reality encounter that sends you spinning. Don't panic, my friend. I believe that as you seek God's answers to the complexities you face, you will be given the wisdom you need to deal constructively with your difficult relationship. In fact, God *promises* in James 1:5, "But if any of you lacks wisdom, let him ask of God, who gives to all men generously and without reproach, and it will be given to him" (NASB).

Cecile determined that she would seek God's wisdom regarding the best course to take with her son, Tracy. As a seventeen-year-old, he was beginning to repeat the folly of his father, a man who had left the family several years before. Tracy had decided that he would do his own thing; no one could tell him anything. He squandered every good opportunity he was offered and was on a fast track to becoming a big-time loser.

His mother had prayed for him all his life, yet it seemed that the fruit of her labor was withering before her very eyes. Cecile needed to know what to do before her son was completely destroyed by his own folly. She prayed, asking for wisdom, and the answer came back loud and clear: *Let Tracy go.*

"But Lord, are you sure? He's still a teenager and so vulnerable!"

Let him go, Cecile.

With an obedient heart but a trembling spirit, this wise woman determined that from that moment on, Tracy was God's challenge to deal with. She stopped trying to direct him and control him. With typical Tracy cockiness and folly, he seemed to run even more wild. That's okay, Cecile told herself. God told me to let him go, and I'm not going to put myself back into the middle of Tracy's whirlwind.

For months there was no change, but then one day Tracy came home a humbled young man. "Mother, may I stay here tonight? I'll leave tomorrow." Cecile welcomed her repentant son and kept praying. Over the next few weeks, Tracy came around more often, demonstrating a changed attitude and a different approach to life. He never explained to his mom what had happened, but something obviously had. Tracy's animosity was gone. The cocky, demanding, demeaning spirit was gone, along with the pleasure that had accompanied his foolish ways. When Cecile obeyed God and got out of his way, God did miracles in young Tracy's life.

Because God works uniquely in everything he does, he doesn't promise that he'll always change the fool in your life; but he does promise to give you wisdom and peace as you seek him. Your goal cannot be to have your fool change; instead, your goal must be to find a personal freedom that allows you to be the person God intends for you to be, no matter what choices your fool makes.

One of the stunning facts you will learn on this journey toward wisdom is that it is not about your beloved fool but about you and all God wants to accomplish in your life. "'For I know the plans I have for you,' declares the LORD, 'plans to prosper you and not to harm you, plans to give you hope and a future. Then you will call upon me and come and pray to me, and I will listen to you. You will seek me and find me when you seek me with all your heart'" (Jeremiah 29:11-13).

In the next section of this book we will explore the ways you tend to compensate for your fool's behavior and what your responses to him do to you as well as to others who share the world in which you live. The realization is going to hit you that relating to a fool is like walking around in a rubber suit. You can't feel what your environment is really like, you can't feel what the touch of another is really like, and you can't move freely in your world. You are confined. The suit is not really protecting you or enabling you to be a more effective person. Rather, it is a hindrance to the real you, and until you take it off, lay it aside, and move on without it, you will never know the freedom of being who God intended you to be!

This is a great point in our journey for you to take a time-out in your learning about yourself and your hard-to-figure person. Set aside what you have learned for a few minutes, take a deep breath, and meditate on the words of Amy Carmichael, a missionary to India who was on the mission field for fifty years. She dealt with many foolish people in extraordinarily difficult situations. She loved the Lord with all her heart and recognized her own impotence apart from him. Her words have always brought encouragement to my heart, and I believe that at this resting spot on our journey, some encouragement from her book *Gold Cord* might be good for you as well:

> We say, then, to anyone who is under trial, give Him time to steep the soul in His eternal truth. Go into the open air, look up into the depths of the sky, or out upon the wideness of the sea, or on the strength of the hills that is His also; or, if bound in the body, go forth in the spirit; spirit is not bound. Give him time and, as surely as dawn follows night, there will break upon the heart a sense of certainty that cannot be shaken.

Linger here awhile until you are ready to go on. The next part of the journey will involve looking at yourself even more honestly and intently. The road ahead may seem a little steep before it gets easier. Soon, though, you'll be in a better place. You won't regret taking the life-giving journey toward wisdom.

If you pay close attention to the fool in your life, you will find that there are certain characteristic behaviors that accompany her wherever she goes. Whether she's interacting with coworkers, grocery clerks, school crossing guards, or her own children, the fool exhibits some predictable kinds of behavior that are the fruit of her thinking. Remember, she is always right, and she trusts in her own heart, so her thinking will influence whatever she does. If she encounters people who think differently than she does, you can be sure she will never question *herself*. Fools believe anyone with a different opinion is automatically wrong. If someone fails to meet her expectations, she will show no mercy.

So, one of the best ways to foolproof your life is to be aware that "foolish is as foolish does." Let's take a closer look at what to watch out for.

Think About It

1. In the margin, note what you think it means to have God's vows upon you. What is the benefit? Do you believe God's vows are on you? If so, why?

   Psalm 56:12-13
   I am under vows to you, O God;
       I will present my thank offerings to you.
   For you have delivered me from death
       and my feet from stumbling,

that I may walk before God
in the light of life.

2. What elements of foolishness do you see that produce fear? Can you remember any time that you were fearful because of your fool? If so, when? How did you get past it, or did you?

Psalm 56:3-6
When I am afraid,
    I will trust in you.
In God, whose word I praise,
    in God I trust; I will not be afraid.
    What can mortal man do to me?
All day long they twist my words;
    they are always plotting to harm me.
They conspire, they lurk,
    they watch my steps,
    eager to take my life.

Go to God About It

1. As you read through the following scriptures, note in the margin what is said about *wickedness* and *evil.* It may be hard for you to equate your fool with those two words, but when you consider that evil is merely opposition to God in one's mind and that wickedness is how the evil is played out in behavior, perhaps it will be a little easier to absorb.

Psalm 5:4-5,8-10

You are not a God who takes pleasure in evil;
    with you the wicked cannot dwell.
The arrogant cannot stand in your presence;
    you hate all who do wrong....
    because of my enemies—
    make straight your way before me.
Not a word from their mouth can be trusted;
    their heart is filled with destruction.
Their throat is an open grave;
    with their tongue they speak deceit.
Declare them guilty, O God!
    Let their intrigues be their downfall.
Banish them for their many sins,
    for they have rebelled against you.

Psalm 7:14-16

He who is pregnant with evil
    and conceives trouble gives birth to disillusionment.
He who digs a hole and scoops it out
    falls into the pit he has made.
The trouble he causes recoils on himself;
    his violence comes down on his own head.

Consult the Bible About It

1. This next psalm is a whole study of what a fool bent on evil will do
   to intimidate. Read it carefully and make note of the behaviors you
   have seen in your fool. Read it a second time and consider whether
   you have seen any of these behaviors in yourself. Behavior tells the
   tale, and you cannot hope to deal honestly with your fool until you
   can be honest about his behavior and yours.

   Psalm 10
   Why, O LORD, do you stand far off?
   > Why do you hide yourself in times of trouble?
   In his arrogance the wicked man hunts down the weak,
   > who are caught in the schemes he devises.
   He boasts of the cravings of his heart;
   > he blesses the greedy and reviles the LORD.
   In his pride the wicked does not seek him;
   > in all his thoughts there is no room for God.
   His ways are always prosperous;
   > he is haughty and your laws are far from him;
   > he sneers at all his enemies.
   He says to himself, "Nothing will shake me;
   > I'll always be happy and never have trouble."
   His mouth is full of curses and lies and threats;
   > trouble and evil are under his tongue.
   He lies in wait near the villages;
   > from ambush he murders the innocent,
   > watching in secret for his victims.
   He lies in wait like a lion in cover;

he lies in wait to catch the helpless;

he catches the helpless and drags them off in his net.

His victims are crushed, they collapse;

they fall under his strength.

He says to himself, "God has forgotten;

he covers his face and never sees."

Arise, LORD! Lift up your hand, O God.

Do not forget the helpless.

Why does the wicked man revile God?

Why does he say to himself,

"He won't call me to account"?

But you, O God, do see trouble and grief;

you consider it to take it in hand.

The victim commits himself to you;

you are the helper of the fatherless.

Break the arm of the wicked and evil man;

call him to account for his wickedness

that would not be found out.

The LORD is King for ever and ever;

the nations will perish from his land.

You hear, O LORD, the desire of the afflicted;

you encourage them, and you listen to their cry,

defending the fatherless and the oppressed,

in order that man, who is of the earth, may terrify no

more.

What Will You Do About It?

1. List the behaviors of your fool that affect you.

2. Since you know you can't change those negative behaviors, why not pray that God will change your fool's behavior or alter the way you are affected by it? Be specific about what you want to see changed. Date the list, and believe by faith that God will move on your behalf.

PART 2

Relating to Your Fool

To show partiality to the wicked is not good,
Nor to thrust aside the righteous in judgment.

PROVERBS 18:5, NASB

To love as Christ loves is to let our love be
a practical and not a sentimental thing.

SIR CHARLES VILLERS STANFORD

Greater love hath no man than this,
that he lay down his friends for his life.

JEREMY THORPE

The ultimate result of shielding men from the effects of folly
is to fill the world with fools.

HERBERT SPENCER

Peace if possible, but truth at any rate.

MARTIN LUTHER

CHAPTER FIVE

Please Excuse My Foolish Loved One

"Denial" is not a river in Egypt, and yet for many of us who are involved with fools, it is our emotional address! Because we love our fools (or at least want to get along with them), we tend to make excuses for them so we can tolerate them and live in some semblance of peace. "Hope springs eternal" in the breast of most people who love a fool, and denial is usually the first line of defense against the pain the fool brings to the relationship. If you can pretend that things aren't as bad as they seem and that there is a compelling reason for his behavior, then it is possible for you to cope while denying there are lifelong behavioral patterns that need to be addressed.

Making excuses and characterizing the fool as a "different" sort of person—one who needs and deserves special consideration—eliminates the need to confront bad behavior and to draw healthy boundaries. If we can excuse our fool, then we can excuse ourselves and our own foolish responses. We don't have to do anything about the chaotic relationship. If we let our fool define the relationship, then there's really not much we have to do. In fact, we tell ourselves there really isn't much we *can* do. We are victims with no options.

Have you ever found yourself coming up with "rational" explanations for your fool's behavior in order to survive emotionally? One common way to do this is to create characteristics for your foolish person that help you excuse him and tolerate the unacceptable behavior. It's easy to slip into a type of denial in which you assign a character role to your foolish individual and view him not so much as a real person who is responsible for his behavior but as a character playing a role he cannot help but play. If you go along with the fool, then you find yourself lost in a plot you were never meant to live, playing a role defined by him. You find that the fool calls the shots and you follow his lead because that seems to be your assigned role in his drama. In this process you run the risk of losing yourself completely.

Below are some common roles we assign our fools in order to excuse their behavior in our own minds and in the minds of other people. See if you recognize any of the following characters in your life's drama.

THE "LOVABLE" ROARING LION

I know a woman who could be crowned the queen of denial. I first became acquainted with this woman I'll call Marilyn many years ago. When I first met her, she was trying to work on her marriage to Ralph. It was the second marriage for both of them. Marilyn had committed her life to Christ and was attending Bible study and earnestly seeking an improved marriage. When Ralph became jealous of her Bible study group, however, Marilyn dropped out of it. Ralph regularly stated he saw nothing wrong with their marriage—other than Marilyn. If she would just catch on to what he needed and what she should be doing, he would be fine!

For years, Marilyn has tried to improve their marriage, and during the majority of that time she has made it better in her mind simply by denying how bad it really is. She never has been able to admit that she is married to a raging fool. When I got to know her, I was appalled to hear Ralph screaming at her as she answered the phone. I have seen her so emotionally beaten down that her health broke. I have watched her little girl grow into a very troubled, anxiety-ridden teenager. I have seen a thriving family business mismanaged into bankruptcy. And through it all, Marilyn's story has been the same. According to her, "Ralph is just a little angry. All of his brothers are that way too. He really means well, but he doesn't know how loud his roar is. He's just a lovable, roaring lion."

As long as she can create an identity for Ralph that casts him as "roaring" yet lovable, Marilyn doesn't have to face the truth that he is a raging, mean, abusive, albeit sometimes charming, man who has gotten no better through her passive acceptance of whatever he's meted out. Denial is a dangerous address when you live with a lovable roaring lion who in reality is a beastly bully seeking to destroy whoever might annoy him. It's easy to tell yourself that you're doing fine in between episodes and to reason with yourself, *What other choice do I have?* But as long as you excuse the lion in your midst, you will forever play the role of the "hunted one" in this bully's dark drama.

THE CHARMER

Golden blond hair, bright blue eyes, and charm that is totally irresistible: these are the qualities Georgia sees in her son, Chase. At age twenty-six he still leads his family through a series of mop-up operations as they try to keep him out of a long-term prison sentence. He uses drugs and regularly gets into fights that "aren't his fault," and yet his beautiful side still hugs his mom, takes his grandmother to the doctor, and smiles brightly when he sees old family friends.

Chase is a con artist, an addict, and a self-absorbed fool. His father, Richard, knows this about his son, and after Chase stole a credit card and ran up a ten-thousand-dollar debt, his dad finally said, "No more." Richard has banned Chase from the house. His mom, on the other hand, just can't stand the thought that this "child" who has cut a destructive swath through their family might be cold or hungry or in need of anything. Even when her grown son's behavior rips her heart out, she holds on to the image of the helpless infant who needs her loving protection.

Georgia is so confused by Chase's good boy–bad boy behavior that she has pushed away her husband, who is deeply disturbed by the whole situation. She has argued with her sisters who have tried to help her, and she has isolated herself from anyone who questions her relationship with her son. She just can't bring herself to draw a line with him because she is so smitten by his charm.

Perhaps you recognize yourself in Georgia. You are not devoid of insight in your relationship to your own fool; it's just that you don't know what to do, and it's easier to believe your beloved difficult person is simply a charmer gone astray. It truly is "easier" to believe that in the short term, but in the long run you will reap destruction if you remain blinded by your fool's manipulation.

THE WAIF

Lorna appears to be kind to all, forgiving, and humble. She endears herself to her colleagues when they first meet because of her gentle, quiet spirit. It doesn't take long, however, for them to feel used and abused because Lorna automatically dons her waif's clothes whenever anything goes wrong. If something looks as if it could get sticky, Lorna retreats into herself and later emerges as a pitiful, needy, whiny adult-child looking for someone to take responsibility for her mess-ups. "Poor me, I am pitiful" is her theme.

She even plays her waif role in the classroom where she teaches second-graders. "Poor Miss Lorna suffers when you children misbehave," she whines. With a puckered pout and a few pathetic sentences she can have the sympathetic little children eating out of her hand. But her behavior has caused the most chaos in her adult friendships. She has had a string of relationships go bad because of her "I am helpless—help me" act.

Juanita is Lorna's latest friend. Juanita told me she feels like the most awful friend in the world because she's so angry at Lorna. She related several incidents when Lorna had arranged for Juanita to take the rap for things that had gone wrong. The latest incident happened at recess. Lorna's class had been particularly unruly one day, so she had asked Juanita if she could join her class with Juanita's during recess. Seeing no problem with the arrangement, Juanita agreed. Ten minutes into the recess period, two of Lorna's students were fighting, and Lorna was nowhere to be found. Juanita was left in charge of all the children, including Lorna's student who got a bloody nose in the fight.

When Juanita finally located Lorna, she was in the teacher's lounge experiencing one of her headaches. "Oh, Juanita, I am so sorry. I told you I was going to run inside the building for a minute, didn't I? (She had not.) I should have told you I wasn't feeling well, but I thought I would just be gone a minute. You will forgive me, won't you?" Once again, Lorna had turned over her own responsibility to an unsuspecting friend. The maddening fact was that she always did it with a reason that was hard to debate.

After this incident, it occurred to Juanita that Lorna has an uncanny ability to twist the facts and play pitiful if things don't go her way. Juanita feels guilty for thinking this way about her friend because she doesn't want to believe that "poor little Lorna" could be so wicked. Since she's never encountered anyone quite like Lorna, Juanita believes that she must be the source of the problem. Lorna blames her, so it must be true. No wonder Juanita feels guilty!

THE PRIMA DONNA

One of the clearest examples I know of the way the companion of a fool suffers harm is the relationship between Will and Serena. Will is an aging pastor who has characterized his wife as a delicate, temperamental prima donna. Serena is indeed unhappy and disturbed, but she is more than delighted when she can play the role of the unpredictable, volatile, and bitter woman. When she plays that role, she keeps at arm's length any people who might expect more of her, she gets what she wants out of Will, and she doesn't have to fulfill her responsibilities as a woman, mother, or pastor's wife.

Serena was born poor, was abused by an older brother, and never felt valued by her parents. She met Will when she was a senior in high school and he was finishing his last year of college. He was good-hearted and merciful and saw Serena, who was also beautiful, as a woman he could love. Serena saw Will as her ticket away from home. Their relationship was rocky from the beginning, but Will, in his mercy, was good to Serena, and she found that the more unhappy she acted the more she got his attention. This unhealthy behavior was established early on, and as a result, thirty-five years and two children later, Will is still meeting Serena at the point of her unhappiness and being controlled by her temperamental ways. In her prima donna role, Serena doesn't have to take any responsibility for the health of her relationships or the well-being of others. No one expects anything from her.

THE MARTYR

Jessie was a bitter, unhappy woman who worked overtime to make sure her two girls were given the best and the most of everything. Ever since they had been tiny she had let them know that they had what they had and were able to do what they wanted only because she had sacrificed for them.

The daughters basically accepted Jessie's version of life and appreciated her in their childlike way—until they reached their teens. Then it began to occur to them that Jessie was a manipulative mother, who played the role of martyr. It dawned on them that Jessie had one person on her mind, and that was Jessie. All of her "sacrificial" actions eventually revolved around her. Either she was clawing to get the credit for what she had done, or she was threatening suicide (and occasionally trying it) in order to prove that even after she had done so much, no one appreciated her!

When I met Jessie's daughters, they were very detached from their mom. They spoke of her as they would speak of a distant, eccentric relative. Because Jessie was always right and believed she could "work out" anything, she had mastered the martyr role. The only problem was that the people she wanted to manipulate into conformity to her will refused to be conformed! A martyr without a cause is an odd character. Relating to such a person is impossible.

You are probably beginning to see the serious problem that assigning roles creates in trying to relate to your difficult person. If the person becomes comfortable with his or her role, then he or she can avoid responsibility and negate any possibility of real relationship. Once this pattern is set up, you are caught.

ROLES, RESPONSIBILITY, AND RELATIONSHIP

When we reach the age where we begin to make things legal and offi-
cial—like getting married, becoming parents, being employed, or holding office—we all have roles to play. Some of us play them well, some
not so well, but there are roles assigned to us just because we are living.
A sixteen-year-old who gives birth is assigned the role of mother whether
or not she is equipped to fulfill it. If everyone around her continues to
treat her as a teenager without any role other than that of being a child,
then that is probably the way she will act.

Similarly, we may play the role of daughter and have the responsibility of a daughter, but if our mothers are fools, then we have no
authentic relationship. Or, if we are married, we may have the role and
responsibility of a wife, but if our mate is a fool, the only relationship we
have is defined by the fool. What we have is an *arrangement* that, at best,
may allow us to "get along." Our role and responsibility stay fairly static,
but any legitimate relationship is chaotic and unattainable. If we fail to
assign the proper roles to the people in our lives and to live with them
in truth, then we operate in a world of unreality. Such a world is a breed-
ing ground for foolish behavior.

Joyce is a thirty-year-old woman who expects her parents to provide
for her the same way they did when she was fifteen. If she moves, she
expects them to be there. If she runs up a credit card bill, she expects
them to pay it. If she's tired or doesn't feel well, she expects them to
understand and plan their schedules accordingly.

Joyce's parents are bright, successful people. They see their other
children as young adults, and that is the role they have assigned to them.
Joyce, however, is their "baby," and throughout her life that role has
stuck. Their thirty-year-old infant sees no need to be responsible or to

cultivate a relationship with her parents based on the adult she really is. Joyce's parents are stuck with how they can respond to their daughter because she is playing the role they have assigned her. Until they change the role assignment, they don't have room for complaint.

One of the hardest hurdles to cross when dealing with your fool is speaking the truth. The first person you must speak truth to is yourself. That is the only way to leave Denial, the dangerous land of smoke and mirrors. As long as you refuse to see your foolish individual for who he is and identify the foolish behavior for what it is, you will never see that person in his proper role and be able to relate in a healthy way. You can play-act with your fool for as long as you want, but until you face the truth, you will always be the one who pays the consequences.

Telling your foolish person the truth can be very much like spitting in the wind. Your words may go nowhere, or they may come back in your face with a splat. But when you have spoken the truth, you stop allowing your foolish person to define you or the situation. This is a turning point. Once you see things as they are, not as you want them to be or as your difficult person tries to define them, you will have new power to foolproof your life. Foolproofing begins with accurately identifying how you are currently responding to your foolish person's behavior and what you are doing to keep the status quo in what can be only a charade of a relationship. As you choose to become more honest about the role your fool plays in your life, you must also be honest about the role you have played in perpetuating your chaotic relationship.

Personally, I have been a master at creating my own reality rather than facing the truth and dealing with it. This has been particularly true in a few very painful relationships. When reality hasn't fit my fantasy, it's been easy for me to come up with a thousand good reasons why things worked out as they did. Once I came to understand what the Bible has to say about the mind-set and behavior of a fool, however, I found that God had already given me permission to admit that something was very wrong and that I didn't have to make it right. No longer did I have to make excuses for the way the difficult people in my life behaved. I was responsible for myself, not for rescuing my fools.

Let me be quick to add that facing the truth makes me no less responsible to be willing to reconcile if there is anything to reconcile. It also doesn't negate my responsibility to forgive. The truth only gives me clear insight into what I'm dealing with so that I don't spin my wheels trying to sustain a fantasy that will never be played out in anything but disappointment and destruction. I no longer have to be at my fools' mercy (or lack thereof!).

Now let's take a deep breath and look at the strategies we may have used to "handle" our fool and the consequences of his behavior. Our own coping strategies can be as subtle, deceitful, and foolish as our fool's, and it's tough to be honest with ourselves. The road ahead may get a little bumpy, but let me encourage you to hang on. There is a smoother trail coming, and you will forever be grateful you made the journey!

GOING DEEPER ON YOUR OWN

An explanation for someone's behavior should never turn into an excuse for the things he does wrong. It is not your job to explain or excuse; to do either puts you in the position of defending your fool's behavior. If you are not in a spot to correct your fool, then your job is to simply allow his behavior to run its course until the consequences are made plain. This is very hard for most of us, because when we stop covering for our fool, the truth about his condition and our situation becomes real. But this is where the healing begins.

Think About It

What part does God play in your life with your fool? Do you think he cares about what happens between you and the fool? Ask yourself the following questions:

1. Have I been completely honest with God about my fool? Why or why not?

2. Do I know what I feel, or have I kept my feelings under wraps by making excuses?

3. Do I believe that things can be different in my life? Why or why not?

4. Is it possible for me to see my fool for who he is and still be okay with myself?

5. Note what God tells you about truth and its significance. Make notes in the margin about what he says, then ask yourself if you are willing to believe him.

Psalm 25:4-6

Show me your ways, O LORD,
    teach me your paths;
guide me in your truth and teach me,
    for you are God my Savior,
    and my hope is in you all day long.

Psalm 145:18

The LORD is near to all who call on him,
    to all who call on him in truth.

Psalm 119:28-32

My soul is weary with sorrow;
    strengthen me according to your word.

Keep me from deceitful ways;
>   be gracious to me through your law.
I have chosen the way of truth;
>   I have set my heart on your laws.
I hold fast to your statutes, O LORD;
>   do not let me be put to shame.
I run in the path of your commands,
>   for you have set my heart free.

Go to God About It

1. In the margin, note what the psalmist is asking of the Lord and what the writer knows about God.

Psalm 17:1-2
Hear, O LORD, my righteous plea;
>   listen to my cry.
Give ear to my prayer—
>   it does not rise from deceitful lips.
May my vindication come from you;
>   may your eyes see what is right.

Psalm 13:3-5
Look on me and answer, O LORD my God.
>   Give light to my eyes, or I will sleep in death;
my enemy will say, "I have overcome him,"
>   and my foes will rejoice when I fall.

But I trust in your unfailing love;

my heart rejoices in your salvation.

I will sing to the LORD,

for he has been good to me.

Proverbs 30:5-6

Every word of God is flawless;

he is a shield to those who take refuge in him.

Do not add to his words,

or he will rebuke you and prove you a liar.

2. Think about how well you know God. Can you say these things about him from personal experience? If so, give a couple of examples.

Consult the Bible About It

Second Samuel 13 tells a sad story of family dysfunction and a father's foolishness. Amnon, Tamar, and Absalom were three children in King David's big family. Amnon was a half-brother to Tamar and Absalom. One day, Amnon got it in his mind that he wanted to have sex with Tamar. He knew she wouldn't be willing to give in to him, so he put together an elaborate plot. He feigned sickness and asked that Tamar be sent to him with some food. When she came into the room, he secured the door, and the following events unfolded.

"Don't, my brother!" she said to him. "Don't force me. Such a thing should not be done in Israel! Don't do this wicked thing. What about me? Where could I get rid of my disgrace? And what about you? You would be like one of the wicked fools in Israel. Please speak to the king; he will not keep me from being married to you." But he refused to listen to her, and since he was stronger than she, he raped her.

Then Amnon hated her with intense hatred. In fact, he hated her more than he had loved her. Amnon said to her, "Get up and get out!"

"No!" she said to him. "Sending me away would be a greater wrong than what you have already done to me."

But he refused to listen to her. He called his personal servant and said, "Get this woman out of here and bolt the door after her." So his servant put her out and bolted the door after her. She was wearing a richly ornamented robe, for this was the kind of garment the virgin daughters of the king wore. Tamar put ashes on her head and tore the ornamented robe she was wearing. She put her hand on her head and went away, weeping aloud as she went. (verses 12-19)

It was a sad day in the palace. Absalom saw what had happened to his sister and began to plot Amnon's murder. King David heard all this, and he was furious. He didn't call Amnon to account as a rapist who had sexually assaulted his daughter. He just got mad. Two years later we see Absalom still plotting Amnon's murder.

Absalom ordered his men, "Listen! When Amnon is in high spirits from drinking wine and I say to you, 'Strike Amnon down,' then kill him. Don't be afraid. Have not I given you this order? Be strong and brave." So Absalom's men did to Amnon what Absalom had ordered. (verses 28-29)

The father of these children was furious, yet he refused to deal with Amnon as the fool that he was! The sad saga of David's family never seemed to be resolved. Absalom took matters into his own hands and killed his brother. The story goes on and on, but for now let's stop and take stock for you.

1. Write out what you see as the consequences you could face for "just being angry" with the fool in your life.

2. How powerful is your anger? What good does it do? Be specific.

3. Why is it important to see your fool for who he really is?

4. Think through what you might do differently in responding to your fool. How could you show more wisdom than King David did?

What Will You Do About It?

Will you ask God to show you the reality of the situation with your fool, the consequences of continuing to "cover" for him, and what God's will for you is at this point? Write out your thoughts in the form of a prayer and date it. As you continue reading this book in the days ahead, return often to this prayer and note what insight the Lord gives you.

Though you pound a fool in a mortar with a pestle
along with crushed grain,
Yet his folly will not depart from him.

PROVERBS 27:22, NASB

There are two kinds of people;
those who say to God, "Thy will be done,"
and those to whom God says, "All right, then, have it your way."

C. S. LEWIS

Be courteous to all but intimate with few,
and let the few be tried.

ABRAHAM LINCOLN

Sometimes one likes foolish people for their folly
better than wise people for their wisdom.

ELIZABETH GASKELL

CHAPTER SIX

A Fool for Love

When you realize that you're beating your head against a wall trying to communicate with your fool, it's easy to become exasperated. Relating to a fool leaves you in the frustrating position of being the one who puts in most of the effort to make the relationship work because the fool is *un*willing to change his or her thinking or behavior. Before long, you usually come up with alternative strategies to deal with him or her, and in the process you find yourself becoming what you never thought you'd be and trying things you never thought you'd try just to "have a relationship."

When we try to relate to a fool over a long period of time and fail to practice the wisdom God offers us, inevitably we begin to think and behave foolishly. When our foolish strategies fail—which they always do because a fool is incapable of relating to us in the way we long for him to—we come to hate who we are and to resent our fool more and more.

In this chapter we'll explore several foolish strategies that those of us who love a fool have tried at one time or another. If you recognize yourself in any of these scenarios, don't despair! An honest self-assessment is the first step toward escaping the dangerous undertow of your pseudo-relationship. You may have become "a fool for love," but real love will enable you to wise up.

STRATEGY 1: PAMPERING

Because of the way a fool thinks, you find that when you talk with him you have no audience unless you say the things he wants to hear. And that is one of the first strategies most people try. If you always agree with your fool and build up his ego, he will usually respond well for a while. If your relationship with him is superficial and there is nothing much at stake but getting along for the moment, then this simple strategy will work. But if this is a family relationship or a work situation that is critical to your career, then you are faced with a dilemma. Do you dare risk the wrath of chaos that will result from speaking the truth? Most people find pampering the fool to be the easier route—at least temporarily.

It is easy to get into a pattern of "tell him what he wants to hear" because there is usually a reward for doing so. You win approval, acceptance, and sometimes material compensation. That's all well and good—until your fool pulls a particularly foolish stunt and your family life or work situation is thrown into chaos.

Lena is a prime example of someone who only wants to hear what she wants to hear. The director of a women's ministry in a large church, Lena is creative, warm, funny, and caring but easily offended if anyone points out a problem. Whoever delivers the message becomes a *persona non grata*. On the surface, Lena will appear to accept what is said and express gratitude, but the person who dared to speak the truth will find herself eliminated from Lena's circle of trusted colleagues. If Lena's control appears to be slipping in any area, she can't stand it. She will quietly but decisively move to regain her grip, no matter whom she has to squash in the process. Consequently, anyone who works with her is in jeopardy.

Dana was an idealistic young woman who looked to Lena as a role model. Quick to anticipate need, Dana was always available to do Lena's bidding without question and with great enthusiasm. She never challenged Lena's sometimes ridiculous requests, and she bent over backward to do what she could to fulfill them.

One particularly trying season, Lena would not settle on the summer plans for the ministry. Several weeks of Lena's on again–off again planning had left her whole staff frazzled. Two quiet secretaries seethed in silence, but knowing Lena's penchant for writing off anyone who questioned her, they didn't dare say anything.

Dana, on the other hand, who had gone far beyond the call of duty for Lena, decided enough was enough. At a particularly stressful staff meeting, Dana said, "Lena, we would be glad to help you, but it seems you really don't know what you want to do." The air became thin as if some invisible being had sucked the oxygen out of the room.

From that moment on, Dana was on her way out the door. Her months of pampering Lena and catering to her every whim had not "worked" to please Lena or to keep Dana's job secure. She had lost Lena's favor, and that was the kiss of death.

STRATEGY 2: POUTING

Pouting is another strategy that it is easy to fall into when you're trying to get your point across to a fool. Donna's father is a fool of the grandest order, but for years when Donna was a teenager and a young woman, she believed she had to please her father and receive positive strokes in return. However, she rarely got them.

When it became clear to Donna that her father didn't care or at least was not going to act as if he cared, she would slip into her childhood habit of pouting and give her father the silent treatment. She claimed she was just "being quiet"; in reality, however, she was pouting in the hope that her father would do an about-face and start acting like he cared. Her pouting was never effective and only kept her in the "child" position with a man who would never give her the approval she craved.

STRATEGY 3: PASSIVITY

Shannon's mother is the fool in her life. From her home six states away, Katherine tries to control her daughter like a marionette on a string. She carefully keeps up with Shannon's plans and uses every opportunity to let her know what she thinks of them. When she disapproves, she rages in a cold, dry-ice fashion. Shannon knows she's done something wrong when Mother cuts off communication and lets the answering machine take Shannon's calls for days at a time. In her heart Shannon knows it's all a game, but she's played it for forty years. Katherine claims great love and motherly affection for her daughter, but she behaves in selfish, manipulative, destructive ways.

Passivity was Shannon's strategy of choice for many years. Whatever her mother said or did, Shannon and her husband, Rex, just let it happen. If her mom wanted to visit, that was fine. If she just wanted to write letters, that was fine. If she wanted to keep the children, that was fine. If she ignored the children, that was fine. Whatever Katherine did, Shannon and Rex accepted as fine.

Eventually Shannon discovered that her inertia only seemed to egg Katherine on toward more control. Katherine became bolder in her invasion of Shannon and Rex's marriage, and when Kelly was born, Katherine treated her like an orphaned puppy she could drag around. She showed up on several occasions and announced that Kelly was coming home with her for the weekend. Neither Shannon nor Rex liked it, but they had been passive for so long that they didn't consider speaking up.

Only when Rex and Shannon began to communicate honestly with each other and form a united front were they able to resist Katherine's control and regain some of their personal sovereignty. Katherine hasn't "gotten it" to this day, but she's realized that she doesn't have permission to invade her daughter's home and control her family. It's taken a long time for Shannon and Rex to wise up, but now they would tell you, "If you're going to be passive, you might as well lie down and die. Being passive just removes the final speed bump for your fool as he plows over you. Passivity is like pouring water on a volcano—useless!"

STRATEGY 4: PROTECTING

Dan and Sue have a very foolish teenage daughter. Jennifer doesn't blink when she lies, rages, and verbally attacks her parents in the hope of gaining the upper hand. For several months both Dan and Sue protected their beloved fool, accepting abuse and deceit in order to have what they called a relationship with Jennifer. They eventually discovered, however, that they did not have a relationship but were being held hostage by a young person determined to have her way. The protection they gave their daughter did nothing but condone her bad behavior.

Finally Dan and Sue were forced, against their own emotional urges, to stop protecting their very bright but foolish child from the consequences of her bad choices. Both have backed out of the protection game, and although the results have not looked good, they believe the consequences could have been worse if they had kept up the pretense of ignoring their daughter's ongoing disrespectful, unacceptable behavior.

Jennifer has ended up in trouble with the law. It remains to be seen which way she will go. When she appears remorseful and seems to learn from her mistakes, her parents are encouraged. When she acts out and stirs up her usual bucket of strife, they get discouraged. Dan and Sue are resigned to the fact that their young fool could go either way, but they do not intend to pay her ticket down the wrong side of "fool's mountain"!

STRATEGY 5: PLEADING

Loraine is a classic fool-lover. She married Gilbert thinking that he would heal the wounds of her fatherless childhood. In the beginning, Gil seemed to be the most wonderful man in the world, but a few years into the marriage he changed. His business was expanding, he was gaining the respect of his peers in the community, and he had less and less time for Loraine. When Loraine tried to talk to him about her feelings, he laughed at her. When she pressed, he became angry. When she suggested counseling, he flatly refused. Finally, when she told him their marriage was in jeopardy, he shrugged her off and replied, "I don't have a problem. I don't know what's wrong with you."

It wasn't long before Loraine changed her tactics. Instead of trying to communicate honestly and directly, she became tearful and childlike, begging him to look at what they were losing. She vacillated between being pitiful and petulant. But no matter what she did, Gilbert was unmoved. Loraine loved Gil deeply and wanted him to love her, but no amount of pleading on Loraine's part kept him from becoming more distant and eventually leaving her for another woman.

Even after Gil left, Loraine held on to her foolish strategy. She continued to write him notes asking, "Don't you remember what we had? Don't you still love me? I still love you!" With a whine in her tone and a tear in her eye, she begged him to be there for her. Sadly, it took Loraine five years to cease and desist in her pleading for Gilbert to return to her. She eventually matured into a woman who could accept her husband's rejection with godly grace. It finally dawned on her that if you have to beg someone to love you, it is possible that you don't have the relationship you think you have.

STRATEGY 6: PLEASING

Sam encountered a fool he never expected. As an idealistic young pastor, Sam wanted to work with a well-known evangelist he had admired for years. When an opportunity came along to be his assistant, Sam jumped at the chance. He couldn't see any downside to his decision. He knew that Pastor Jones was very effective with the congregations where he preached. Sam believed he could help this great man become even greater as he worked alongside him.

When he interviewed for the job, Sam was told that two men had left the ministry who just couldn't do the job the pastor needed to have done. Sam assured Pastor Jones, "You can count on me!" Unfortunately, in a few months the glow was gone, and Sam was feeling the crush of the pastor's control. He had to answer for how he spent his time away from work, how he spent his money, and who his friends were. At first he was flattered by the pastor's interest and concern. Sam didn't have a father, and this seemed like fatherly interest. He drank it in and reciprocated by working outrageous hours to please his boss.

One day the pastor lost his temper (not for the first time), and Sam finally acknowledged some things he hadn't been wanting to see. It was so hard to face the fact that he had been drawn into a tight relationship with a man who would not be questioned, who demanded control, and who used anger to get his way. Sam's idealism lay at his feet, but his determination to make things work pushed him relentlessly to try to please the pastor. He tried to talk with him but was rebuffed. He tried to enlist the help of another pastor who was a friend to both of them, but Sam was called a "Judas" for saying there was a problem. He searched his own heart and even blamed himself for not "honoring" his boss, this respected man of God, more highly. On he slogged, enduring the pastor's distance and anger and working overtime to get the job done to the man's satisfaction. Of course, he never did. When an opportunity to join an overseas mission organization came his way, Sam took it as his way of escape. Burned out and wounded by trying to please a fool, Sam had lost respect for himself and trust in people in power.

STRATEGY 7: PRODDING

If Jake was ever going to amount to anything, Gloria decided it would be through her prodding. A promising artist, Jake was the kind of guy who was stubborn one day and lovable the next and who had convinced himself (and her) that he couldn't work for anyone because bosses "just didn't understand" him. His quick temper and opinionated comments had left him without steady work.

Gloria believed that she could help her husband "be all that he could be" if she just stayed behind him. She convinced herself that he could be a well-known artist if someone would just believe in him and keep him motivated. Well, she did, and he isn't! Gloria staked her claim on a fool who, because he was always right in his own eyes and quick to let the world know how right he was, could not support her and their children. She had taken on that job herself, along with the one of being Jake's holy prod—a job she could have for a lifetime! That suited Jake just fine.

ARE YOU A FOOL FOR LOVE?

If you still have doubts about whether or not you're relating to a fool and possibly becoming "a fool for love" in the process, try making a list of

"This is what I feel" statements. I suggest that you look at your feelings so you can understand how facts are distorted by relating to your fool.

This exercise will require some thought and time. As you begin to put it down on paper, you may be amazed at the profile that emerges. If you get stumped on the "I feel" messages, then look at the partial list below and see if you can recognize what has been going on with you.

I feel…

- inadequate in most situations.
- guilty, although I can't pinpoint a specific reason.
- as if I have to check in with someone (my fool) before I can make a decision.
- as if I have to protect my fool and protect other people from my fool.
- as if I must protect my heart from my fool.
- as if there is a shadow across my relationship with God.

If you will look honestly at what you're feeling, you'll see that you're letting your fool define you. By being entangled with your fool you have become what you never thought you would be: a controlled person. The first step toward change comes when you discover the truth that you do not have a relationship; rather, *you have an arrangement*. You have learned to survive this sad reality by strategically reacting, albeit foolishly, to the difficult person with whom you desire meaningful interaction.

Eventually you will come to a defining moment—a time when your situation becomes clear, when your fool emerges from behind the veil in which you have cloaked him, and when there is opportunity to seek wisdom as never before. Torn between being foolish yourself and recognizing that you've been scratching in red clay looking for the gold of relationship, you're ready to look at yourself and the person you have become.

Pouring water on a duck's back is the equivalent of your effort to change your fool. It is wasted effort with no results. Your fool is an expert at "explaining" what he thinks without stopping to consider anything you or anyone else might have to say. If there is to be a satisfactory outcome to your dilemma with your fool, then you must turn your focus on yourself and what can be changed in *you*.

I cannot count the scores of people I have listened to as they've explained what they've done to make their situation with their fool more tolerable. One woman I talked with said, "I'm working three jobs because my fool won't work." A defeated man said, "I just keep taking care of our kids while my wife goes from affair to affair." When I asked him why, he said, "My daddy always told me 'God hates divorce,' and I'm afraid that my church would disown me if I left my wife."

"How many affairs has she had?" I asked.

"Six that I know about. She says she wants to stay married, but she keeps ending up in someone else's bed and expects me to just take it. It's killing me!"

When I listen to these sad tales, the question that always comes to my mind is, *What will it take for this "companion of a fool" to stop doing the same things over and over again?* A wise person's definition of insanity is "doing the same thing over and over and expecting different results." My heart cries out, *When will you stop giving your life away in little pieces? When will you assume responsibility for the life God has given you?* The only way to foolproof your life is to stop being foolish yourself.

Think About It

1. Name at least two things you have done in relating to your fool that you never thought you would do.

2. How do you feel when you do these things you never planned to do?

3. This is honesty time. How do you rationalize doing the things you never thought you would do or doing the things you hate?

4. If you were God, how would you view the strategies you have used to change or influence your fool?

Go to God About It

1. When you hang around a fool, one of the greatest dangers is becoming like him or her. Think about that fact as you meditate on this passage from Ecclesiastes.

Ecclesiastes 5:1-7

Guard your steps when you go to the house of God. Go near to listen rather than to offer the sacrifice of fools, who do not know that they do wrong.

Do not be quick with your mouth,
>   do not be hasty in your heart
>   to utter anything before God.
God is in heaven
>   and you are on earth,
>   so let your words be few.
As a dream comes when there are many cares,
>   so the speech of a fool when there are many words.

When you make a vow to God, do not delay in fulfilling it. He has no pleasure in fools; fulfill your vow. It is better not to vow than to make a vow and not fulfill it. Do not let your mouth lead you into sin. And do not protest to the temple messenger, "My vow was a mistake." Why should God be angry at what you say and destroy the work of your hands? Much dreaming and many words are meaningless. Therefore stand in awe of God.

2. Read the passage again, making notes in the margin about "the sacrifice of fools." What is it?

3. How can you avoid making the same sacrifice?

Consult the Bible About It

Comparing and contrasting is one of the ways the Bible communicates word pictures. Find every comparison or contrast you can in the following verses and note what a fool is like and what a man of understanding or a wise man is like. Jot your notes in the margin.

Proverbs 10:8

The wise in heart accept commands,

    but a chattering fool comes to ruin.

Proverbs 10:23

A fool finds pleasure in evil conduct,

    but a man of understanding delights in wisdom.

Proverbs 15:2

The tongue of the wise commends knowledge,

    but the mouth of the fool gushes folly.

Proverbs 26:5

Answer a fool according to his folly,

    or he will be wise in his own eyes.

Proverbs 26:6

Like cutting off one's feet or drinking violence
  is the sending of a message by the hand of a fool.

Proverbs 26:7

Like a lame man's legs that hang limp
  is a proverb in the mouth of a fool.

Proverbs 26:8

Like tying a stone in a sling
  is the giving of honor to a fool.

Proverbs 26:9

Like a thornbush in a drunkard's hand
  is a proverb in the mouth of a fool.

Proverbs 26:10

Like an archer who wounds at random
  is he who hires a fool or any passer-by.

Proverbs 26:11

As a dog returns to its vomit,
  so a fool repeats his folly.

Proverbs 26:12

Do you see a man wise in his own eyes?
  There is more hope for a fool than for him.

It is as if the writer of these proverbs is saying, "What is it about 'fool' that you don't understand?"

What Will You Do About It?

Take a moment to write out what you believe God would have you do about your fool at this point in your journey. Are you willing to acknowledge that nowhere in Scripture are you told to do anything to change your fool? If you can come to that conclusion, you will have made a quantum leap to the next phase of your journey.

He who walks with wise men will be wise,
But the companion of fools will suffer harm.

PROVERBS 13:20, NASB

That's the penalty we have to pay for our acts of foolishness—
someone else always suffers for them.

ALFRED SUTRO

Never be ashamed to own that you have been in the wrong,
'tis but saying you are wiser today than you were yesterday.

JONATHAN SWIFT

Every moment of one's existence
one is growing into more or retreating into less.
One is always living a little more
or dying a little bit.

NORMAN MAILER

CHAPTER SEVEN

The Fool in the Mirror

Sharon slammed her fist on the table as she spoke of her ex-husband's outrageous comments. She hated what he was, how he was behaving, and how he was influencing their teenage children. She felt helpless, hopeless, and totally outraged by his antics. The redness in her cheeks revealed her agitation. Her words were sharp, bitter, and full of anger. She looked like an animal who was cornered in a cage. Like the movie character swinging at the much larger tough guy he just can't reach, Sharon was swinging at her circumstances, expending her energy, and making herself sick while nothing was changing. Her anger was explosive.

She didn't know what to do about the situation or about herself. "I want to do what is right, and I hate what I have become!" she cried. Burying her head in her hands, she sobbed, "What am I going to do? What am I going to do?"

Sharon had not started out as an angry person. She was the typical "let's get along" kind of girl when she had met Chris. He was angry occasionally, but she didn't take it seriously because he seemed like such a sweetheart the rest of the time. What she failed to recognize was that he was angry when things didn't go his way, and if she could fix whatever displeased him, then he quit being angry. She rescued him many times just to keep the peace. Whether it was with his family, her family, or the neighbors, if Chris got himself into a corner with his anger, Sharon smoothed it over.

There is a principle in the Scriptures that Sharon didn't know, so she didn't realize she was setting herself up for future heartache. That principle is this: "A man of great anger shall bear the penalty, for if you rescue him, you will only have to do it again" (Proverbs 19:19, NASB). The longer Chris and Sharon were together, his anger increased. She covered for him, and the next time she had to cover more. Over time, Chris developed into a man of great anger.

Sharon was fearful of his outbursts and embarrassed by the things he would say and do. She began declining family functions whenever possible and opted to "just stay home" if anything came up where she and Chris might have to attend together. It was easier to stay away. She could handle him at home, but she couldn't deal with him in public.

As Chris became more difficult, Sharon's heart began to harden. She knew it, hated it, but didn't do anything about it. Her hardness was her defense against Chris's outbursts. She tried to pray for him, but that made her angry. Then she prayed for herself, but she was so angry she felt her prayers were bouncing off the ceiling. Sharon was experiencing the truth of the second principle she didn't know: "Do not associate [be in the same pasture] with a man given to anger; or go with a hot-tempered man, lest you learn his ways, and find a snare for yourself" (Proverbs 22:24-25, NASB).

Sharon was snared. She was angry, just like Chris. And she used her anger with just as much ferocity. She had learned his ways, and in grabbing hold of a weapon that she didn't know how to use, she was hurting herself and other people.

Sharon had made two common mistakes, and she was reaping a common result. She had tried to rescue Chris from the consequences of his anger, and she had continued to be associated with him in the midst of his anger. By not separating herself from his outrage, she had become enraged. Now she was recognizing the woman she had become, and she hated her!

MIRROR, MIRROR ON THE WALL

I recently talked with a group of people who have found balanced, healthy lifestyles after realizing they were allowing themselves to be controlled by their fools. I asked, "What did you become when you were allowing your fool to define you?" (They knew what I meant by *your fool* and *define* because we had worked on their issues with their fools for some time.) I was overwhelmed with their honesty! One woman seemed to sum it up best when she said, "I knew I was in trouble when I became selfish, when I felt I had to lie just to get through whatever upheaval we were involved in. And then I became sick; I was physically sick all the time. They weren't major illnesses but the kinds of infections that lay you low. I knew enough about life to recognize that my body, soul, and spirit were being destroyed, little by little."

Each person I talked with painted a picture of someone he or she did not like, someone who had abdicated to another's image of them, and they were ashamed of the result. These people never meant to turn out this way, but through the steady friction of rubbing against their fools, the result was evident, and they had reached the point where they knew something had to change.

A doctor friend of mine described what had happened to them this way: "When you relate to a fool, it's not just irritating or abrasive; it will

you are. I work on furniture, and if I want to get rid of small
imperfections or smooth out a rough place, I use a fine sandpaper, something that is coated with many small, fine grains. I think of those abrasive
grains of sand as the people God uses in our lives to help us grow. Their
presence is a challenge that we are better for having overcome. They are
people who are different than we are, and as we emotionally rub against
them, they help us get rid of some of our imperfections. We can be better
for having interacted with them even if the situation wasn't pleasant.

"There's another kind of paper, and that's the kind that alters the
very appearance and contour of a piece of wood. If I want to change
what this wood looks like, then I get out the coarse paper. It has very few
grains, but the grains that are there are large and powerful. With a few
swipes of the paper I can do some major damage. That's what relating to
a fool is all about."

It was interesting to me that none of the people I talked with said that
while they were in the thick of their involvement with their fools they
were truthful, caring, kind, loving, or spiritual. And there is a reason for
that. When you allow a fool to define who you are and you fail to correct
his definition, you become the exact representation of who the fool says
you are. If you are called "stupid" and you believe it, then you can act
stupidly! If you are called "crazy" and you believe it, then you take on the
behavior of someone who is crazy. You see, part of the tragedy of continuing to engage a fool is that, despite all of your protestations and efforts
to alter him, *you* are the one who will be altered—and not for the better!

Attempting to relate to your fool is time-consuming and exhausting.
Remember, a fool will give you no rest (see Proverbs 29:9). And if you have
no rest, then your mind becomes muddled. It is hard to make a decision.
It is hard to think about anything except what your fool is doing or saying.

So you can see why beginning to focus on yourself car
almost have to peel your eyes off your fool even to se
self other than how you are affected by his behavior

If you are entangled with a fool and you are feeling like a pie
soft pine that has been altered, scarred, and indelibly changed by the
coarse sandpaper of your fool's defining work, there is hope for you. Just
as a fool's tool is *foolishness*, so the instrument you can command is
understanding! When you *understand*, you will be able to see things as
they are and respond appropriately.

THE WAY OF UNDERSTANDING

One of the first "things as they are" facts you need to learn is that it is
impossible to correct, change, alter, redefine, censure, sweet-talk, or
reason with a fool. Let me say that again: *It is impossible.* If you take
nothing else away from this chapter, then at least hang on to this truth:
If you try to change your fool, you will fail! Get that, my friend, and get
it well. If you do, then you will be able to successfully foolproof your life.

The Bible says, "Understanding is a fountain of life to him who has
it, but the discipline of fools is folly" (Proverbs 16:22, NASB). In other
words, *any attempt to correct a fool is useless* because "discipline" is foolishness to one who despises wisdom, mocks at guilt, and starts quarrels.
This is the great dividing line: If discipline does nothing to change the
fool, then your focus must be on you and your "understanding."
Wisdom must become your goal and your hope. It must be your safe
haven and your delight.

If you can gain understanding, you will have a fountain of life, and
that's what facing the truth about yourself and your fool is all about. The
word *understanding* means "wisdom, insight, and good sense." The word

ntain means "spring, a source of life, of joy and purification." The word *life* implies "lively or active." So let's put that all together to explain this truth: If you have wisdom, you will have a source of life within you that will make you lively and active. Think about it. You have to be fully alive to be lively and active, but most people who relate to a fool on an ongoing basis become like Sharon at the beginning of this chapter: helpless, hopeless, and spiritually and emotionally sick.

Once you fully recognize that you are relating to a fool, then you can begin to shift your strategies. No longer is your fool in charge. You cannot change what your fool says or does, but you do not have to give him ownership of your feelings or behavior. You can be in control of who you are, of who you become, and of the way you live your life. That may be a novel concept for you, yet if you will begin to roll it around in your mind, you will discover renewed hope and joy!

One of the things we learn in life is that circumstances rarely change dramatically; so if you are going to be a person of understanding, it will have to be in your own heart—not in the midst of a big change in your situation. You will still see your fool, talk to your fool, and if you're married to him or her, you will continue to sleep with your fool. So please understand that there may not be a big change in your circumstances. Rather, the big change will be in you!

Sometimes in life we face incredibly complex situations—some created by our fools, some by our own lack of wisdom. All are allowed by God for a greater purpose in our lives. But when we assume that we have no choices and that our fools are in charge, it's easy to waste our lives away wondering what to do next or grieving because we feel we have no options. That's where understanding becomes critical; it's also a good place to meet Abigail.

A WOMAN OF WISDOM

This is a great story about someone who knew that she could do nothing to change her fool, but neither did she allow her fool to define her. She was not a self-centered, self-trusting woman. She was a woman of understanding who did what was right to preserve her household.

Abigail is remembered for her gracious handling of a very touchy situation between her husband, Nabal, and King David. A title for this whole stressful scenario might be "Nabal's My Name; Foolishness Is My Game." Let me fill you in on some of the details straight from Scripture, and I think you will see the wisdom Abigail possessed.

The story begins in 1 Samuel 25:3 with the writer's description of a perfectly mismatched couple. Abigail is described as "an intelligent and beautiful woman." Her dear husband, on the other hand, had some social deficits. He is described as "surly and mean in his dealings." He also seemed to be determined to live up to his name. Nabal means "fool." We don't know if his mother just knew what her boy would be or if she saw these tendencies early on and gave him the label then. At any rate, Nabal was a good businessman and made lots of money, but he failed miserably in the "decent human being" category.

There was a custom in that day that if you saw someone's property or encountered someone's enterprise, the gallant thing to do was to leave them alone without harming them (without relieving them of any of their goods) and to protect them at the same time. It was sort of a dual service: I won't mess with your stuff, and I won't let anyone else do it either!

King David, the man after God's own heart, happened on Nabal's business enterprises and immediately told his men to protect Nabal's men while they were shearing their sheep and to do them no harm. The other part of the custom was that when you rendered such a service, the kindness was returned, and the one you had protected took care of you with food, supplies, and gifts.

Thinking Nabal would be a neighborly fellow, King David sent his men to tell Nabal who they were and what they had done for him. The message he sent was this: "Have a long life, peace be to you, and peace be to your house, and peace be to all that you have."

Well, David's message of peace apparently did not impress Nabal, because this was his response: "Who is David? And who is the son of Jesse? There are many servants today who are each breaking away from his master. Shall I then take my bread and my water and my meat that I have slaughtered for my shearers, and give it to men whose origin I do not know?" (verses 10-11, NASB).

Uh-oh! When King David heard these words, he was angry. He told his men to grab their swords, and he grabbed his as well, and with a force of about four hundred men he marched off to teach Nabal some manners.

One of the young men who had been protected by David's men remembered his manners, however, and knew he didn't want to get in this fight. So he ran for his mistress, Abigail. He reported to her that David's men had been great but that Nabal had been rude. He told her, "The men were very good to us, and we were not insulted, nor did we miss anything as long as we went about with them, while we were in the fields. They were a wall to us both by night and by day, all the time we were with them tending the sheep" (verses 15-16, NASB).

But things had changed now, the man told Abigail, explaining that David's men were plotting to take out Nabal and his whole family. With timid pleading but enormous respect for Abigail, the young man said, "Now therefore know and consider what you should do, for evil is plotted against our master and against all his household; and he is such a worthless man that no one can speak to him" (verse 17, NASB).

Now we see the problem: We have a fool on our hands, and King David is out to correct the fool's inhospitable, boorish, self-centered behavior. Fortunately, the wisdom of Abigail prevailed. She got busy gathering supplies and sent the young man ahead of her. She didn't mention anything to Nabal but loaded her donkeys and headed out to meet David as he approached with his troops to obliterate Nabal.

King David was *very* angry. He had encountered a fool and had not taken to the encounter kindly…but then Abigail showed up—wise, understanding Abigail!

"When Abigail saw David, she hurried and dismounted from her donkey, and fell on her face before David, and bowed herself to the ground. And she fell at his feet and said, 'On me alone, my lord, be the blame. And please let your maidservant speak to you, and listen to the words of your maidservant. Please do not let my lord pay attention to this worthless man, Nabal, for as his name is, so is he. Nabal is his name and folly is with him; but I your maidservant did not see the young men of my lord whom you sent" (verses 23-25, NASB).

Abigail was a woman of understanding. She knew the facts, faced the facts, and did what she had to do. Remember, our dear king was just about ready to wipe out her whole household! This was a woman caught between a foolish husband and a king with a score to settle. Not a good position for anyone! But she quickly began to unload the supplies and food she had brought and gave them to David to appease what in that day and in that culture could be interpreted as a righteous anger.

Then David said to Abigail, "Blessed be the LORD God of Israel, who sent you this day to meet me, and blessed be your discernment, and blessed be you, who have kept me this day from bloodshed, and from avenging myself by my own hand" (verse 32, NASB). Abigail had saved the day. David sent her back to her home in peace, and I can just see her young servant breathing a sigh of relief as the great king turned on his horse and led his four hundred men out of the camp.

Abigail had to go back and tend to things with her foolish, harsh, evil husband. He was so consumed with his feasting and merrymaking that he had no idea his wife had just averted total disaster for him and his family! He was drunk, so he was in no frame of mind to talk about it.

Abigail said nothing about what had happened until the next morning. Then, groggy from the night before, Nabal could not believe what Abigail was telling him. He was shocked, so shocked that he had a heart attack or a stroke; the Bible doesn't specify which. It only reports that "his heart failed him," and he became like a stone. Ten days later, he died.

Not one to miss an opportunity to marry another beautiful wife, when the news arrived in David's camp that Nabal, the fool, was dead, the king said, "Blessed be the LORD, who has pleaded the cause of my reproach from the hand of Nabal" (verse 39, NASB). Then he sent a message to Abigail, saying in essence, "By the way, Abigail, I like your style. Would you be my wife?"

This is a good place to stop and ponder the fact that this story had two strong-willed men who both, at one point, were ready to fight. Nabal was belligerent and wanted to be in control of the whole scenario. He was a suspicious, self-centered fool. David was going to fight because he was right! He had done his duty by being "a wall" for Nabal's men. Because Nabal had rebuffed him, fighting was the recourse David hastily chose. When it came down to lining up for the battle, neither man was on a righteous mission. A lot of pride was at stake, and it took Abigail, a woman of discernment, to defuse the situation.

FACING YOUR OWN FOOLISHNESS AND FEARS

You may not have someone as foolish as Nabal in your life, but whoever your difficult person is, you know that dealing with him feels like an uphill battle. When you start taking an honest look at your twisted relationship, it's easy to think, *This relationship is impossible!* At the moment, this may seem like a truthful statement based on all you know about the interactions between you and your fool. But hopelessness, despair, and futility may be clouding the picture.

Perhaps you have forgotten that someone else is on the scene besides your fool: *you!* And you are not hopeless! You have probably taken on some foolish behaviors in response to your fool; maybe you've become sullen or demanding, controlling or pathetic. I know you hate that, but the disgust you feel toward yourself and your situation can become a good thing if you are appalled enough to give up your futile strategies in order to seek a better way to relate to your fool.

As you begin to focus on yourself, be careful that you don't get bogged down in regret, self-recrimination, self-pity, or anger. It would be so easy to look at how you feel and then become sad and pitiful because you've awakened to the fact that your life has been made extremely difficult by your fool. Don't succumb, my friend. You don't need to become introspective and depressed but rather contemplative and humble as you consider what wisdom God offers for your journey toward emotional and spiritual recovery.

Your first response to facing reality will probably be fear. You may find that being honest about who you've become and considering a change in the way you behave with your fool threatens your security. You may fear that your fool will not want you around anymore if you quit pampering or protecting or even pouting. You may be told that you've changed (and not for the better!). You will be tested to see if you are really going to act wisely or if you can be cajoled into responding the way your fool wants you to respond. You will probably be bribed, verbally attacked, shamed, or made to feel guilty. Your emotions will be up and down, and at times you will be tempted to quit and just let things stay as they are. But that won't work. The undertow of your difficult relationship is slowly pulling you away from the shore of sanity. You have to hang on and fight your way back. This may sound extreme, but if you've been near drowning in a relationship with a fool, you know it's true.

The Lord is with you. He promises to sustain you and fill you with the wisdom you need. He himself dealt with fools while he lived on earth, and In no situation did he alter the truth in order to deal with a difficult person. He never denied someone's foolish behavior in order to gain acceptance. Many of the people he rubbed shoulders with were religious, self-possessed, and out to kill him. With some of them he remained silent; with others he spoke with bold clarity. But nowhere in Scripture will you find Jesus, the God-man, altering truth in order to mollify the person with whom he was relating.

If you decide to face the whole truth of your situation and live in the light of it, your confusion will dissipate, and the wise path will become clear. The journey certainly may be painful, because truth clears away not only the clouds of obscurity but the pillows of comfort as well. You must remember, however, that to remain in the vice of a fool's grip will eventually destroy the person you could be. Your journey toward wisdom may be an ordeal at times, but I promise you it will also be a glorious adventure.

This is the hardest time in the whole course you are on. This is the moment when you lay down your plans, your schemes, your defense mechanisms, and most importantly, you lay down the lies! You are no longer willing to allow your fool, whoever he or she may be, to define you. You have faced the fact that you cannot define or alter your difficult person. If you truly are willing to try to live in the light of these truths, then you, my friend, are ready to move on. You are ready to make a big leap beyond your present existence. You are making marvelous progress, and I commend you!

"May my cry come before you, O LORD; give me understanding according to your word" (Psalm 119:169). Understanding is the quality you need the most when you turn away from trying to change your fool or change yourself for your fool. Wisdom is knowledge of God and his ways. Understanding is the ability to apply that wisdom to your everyday life. Now that you have turned your focus on yourself and the truth you need to assimilate, you can gain understanding. A good place to start is with identifying the lies you have believed. Once you know where you have lacked wisdom, you can begin to change your life for the better.

Think About It

I'll start a "Lies I Have Believed" list for you, and you can add to it.

1. I can do something to change my fool.
2. I am responsible for my fool's thinking and behavior.
3. I owe it to God to keep trying to alter, change, nurture, or fix my fool.
4. I can't be a good Christian if I don't try to help my fool.
5. I don't deserve anything better than what my fool is giving because I'm not perfect either.
6.

7.

8.

9.

10.

Go to God About It

1. Read the following scriptures and meditate on what God is saying to you, personally. Make notes to yourself in the margin.

Psalm 25:4-5

Show me your ways, O LORD,

 teach me your paths;

guide me in your truth and teach me,

 for you are God my Savior,

 and my hope is in you all day long.

Psalm 51:6

Surely you desire truth in the inner parts;

 you teach me wisdom in the inmost place.

Psalm 86:11-17

Teach me your way, O LORD,

 and I will walk in your truth;

give me an undivided heart,

 that I may fear your name.

I will praise you, O Lord my God, with all my heart;

 I will glorify your name forever.

For great is your love toward me;

 you have delivered me from the depths of the grave.

The arrogant are attacking me, O God;
>   a band of ruthless men seeks my life—
>   men without regard for you.
> But you, O Lord, are a compassionate and gracious God,
>   slow to anger, abounding in love and faithfulness.
> Turn to me and have mercy on me;
>   grant your strength to your servant
>   and save the son of your maidservant.
> Give me a sign of your goodness,
>   that my enemies may see it and be put to shame,
>   for you, O LORD, have helped me and comforted me.

2. As you read, try to put together a definition of what you would call "an undivided heart." Write it down here.

3. Do you have an undivided heart? If so, how do you know? If not, how do you know that?

Consult the Bible About It

In the margin, mark the "who, what, when, where, and why's" of the passage. Then answer the questions at the end of the passage.

Psalm 145:13-19

The LORD is faithful to all his promises
   and loving toward all he has made.
The LORD upholds all those who fall
   and lifts up all who are bowed down.
The eyes of all look to you,
   and you give them their food at the proper time.
You open your hand
   and satisfy the desires of every living thing.
The LORD is righteous in all his ways
   and loving toward all he has made.
The LORD is near to all who call on him,
   to all who call on him in truth.
He fulfills the desires of those who fear him;
   he hears their cry and saves them.

1. To what is God faithful?

2. To whom is he loving?

3. Whom does the Lord uphold?

4. Whom does he lift up?

5. Whom does he feed?

6. Whose desires does he satisfy?

7. What characterizes all of the Lord's ways?

8. To whom is God near?

9. What does truth have to do with it?

10. What does God do for those who fear him?

11. What does he do when they cry?

If the Lord is so tuned in to you and your inmost needs, isn't it time to consider how you relate to a God who cares for you this much? If you are a believer who has been consumed with your fool, the following scripture will be like a breath of fresh air as you read it and personalize it, as I've done by changing the pronouns.

What, then, shall I say in response to this? If God is for me, who can be against me? He who did not spare his own Son, but gave him up for me—how will he not also, along with him, graciously give me all things? Who will bring any charge against those whom God has chosen? It is God who justifies. Who is he that condemns? Christ Jesus, who died—more than that, who was raised to life—is at the right hand of God and is also interceding for me. Who shall separate me from the love of Christ? Shall trouble or hardship or persecution or famine or nakedness or danger or sword? As it is written:

"For your sake I face death all day long;

I am considered as sheep to be slaughtered."

No, in all these things I am more than a conqueror through him who loved me. For I am convinced that neither death nor life, neither angels nor demons, neither the present nor the future, nor any powers, neither height nor depth, nor anything else in all creation, will be able to separate me from the love of God that is in Christ Jesus my Lord. (Romans 8:31-39)

What Will You Do About It?

Write a prayer of gratitude to the Lord who has loved you dearly and faithfully while you have been so absorbed with your fool. He deserved to be first in your life, but being entangled with your fool may have dimmed your view of how much he loves you and how much you love him. Thank him for his gracious patience and his steadfast love.

PART 3

WISEN UP

Folly is bound up in the heart of a child,
but the rod of discipline will drive it far from him.

PROVERBS 22:15

Be wise with speed;
A fool at forty is a fool indeed.

EDWARD YOUNG

Growth begins when we begin to accept our own weaknesses.

JEAN VANIER

A child becomes an adult when he realizes
that he has a right not only to be right
but also to be wrong.

THOMAS SZASZ

CHAPTER EIGHT

Putting Away Childish Things

Dealing with a fool can and will consume all of your time and all of your effort if you let it. Whether you have given birth to your fool or whether you have married your fool or whether your fool works next to you at the office, the dilemmas are similar. The fool soon becomes the focus of your attention. Fools just have a way of making themselves the whirling force around which everyone else must twist and twirl in order to stay afloat. If you think about it, it doesn't take long to see that you are being influenced rather than influencing. Very quickly you will realize that your joy and well-being are affected by the behavior of your fool and that the focus of your life is altered.

"My son is a fool," Kathleen said with tears in her eyes but with resolution in her voice. "His fortieth birthday was last week, and to be honest with you, something snapped in me. Maybe I just woke up! My son has had every advantage a kid could have. We have loved him, tried to educate him, given him extra help and many privileges. We have talked with him for hours, just 'being there' when he wanted to talk. Yet none of that ever seems to help. He still cannot or will not get a job that he will stay with for any length of time. Someone is always 'giving him a hard time.' He has dabbled in a little of this and a little of that, but he just hasn't found his niche. He has turned his life over to Christ, involved himself in church, and then fallen away. We had great hope for change when he did that. But today it hit me: *He is a fool.* So what do I do now?"

Over the years I had talked many times with Kathleen about her son Josh. I have even talked with Josh. He is charming, but he is always in a mess. His first wife finally gave up on him. His second wife has been separated from him for two years. His brothers and sisters have very little to do with him, and yet he is still his mother's son. He is a human being with potential locked up somewhere in his self-possessed bubble.

His dad died several years ago, but from the time Josh was fifteen, Kathleen and her husband had been looking for the cure for Josh. It was at that point they realized Josh had not developed like his brothers and sisters had. He had become angry and manipulative and seemed unable to "find himself" anywhere. He was capable of learning but wouldn't. He was able to work but chose to pick what would be suitable for him. He was a charmer a great deal of the time but often became morose. Josh's world revolved around him.

So, what to do? With what options do fools leave you? As we've already established, you cannot change them. You must remember that your hope is in God and his plan for you and your fool. Since your hope is not in changing your fool through manipulation or even Christian kindness, you must take your focus off your fool and turn it on yourself. When you do, you will no doubt see your own anger and futile strategies, your own pain and fear. And you will probably begin to recognize your own immaturity in the ways you've chosen to think about and relate to your fool. It's time to wise up.

CHILDISH BEHAVIOR

Friday afternoon in Atlanta's Hartsfield International Airport is always an adventure. One autumn Friday in 1994 was no different. I was flying Kiwi Airlines to a speaking engagement in Florida. The gate area was full of travelers enjoying the idea that we had discovered such a great reduced fare for the journey. Everyone's joy turned to disappointment, however, when it was announced there would be a two-hour delay before we could take off for Florida.

Despite the long wait, there was a minimum of complaining among the passengers, until one rather short man with an ill-fitting toupee stood in the center of the gate area and announced for all to hear, "I am *the biggest attorney in Atlanta,* and I want you all to join me in a class-action suit against Kiwi Airlines." Those of us who were in the area watched in astonishment as he stood like Peter Pan waiting to lead all of us on a self-serving journey with him, *the biggest attorney in Atlanta,* as our self-appointed leader! He was deflated rather quickly, however, when a woman in the crowd called him down in her most exasperated motherly tone. "Why don't you just sit down and shut up?" More amazing than his pronouncement was the way he obediently sat down. We didn't hear another word from *the biggest attorney in Atlanta* for the rest of our trip!

Most of us in the gate area that day were fully aware we were experiencing an inconvenience over which we had no control, and we were willing to take it in stride. *The biggest attorney in Atlanta,* however, had another agenda. He did not like what was happening. He was being inconvenienced, and someone was going to pay for causing *him* to wait. Not only that, he was going to say whatever he wanted to say in order to express his displeasure. It didn't matter how hard the airline personnel were working to get us airborne. He was going to have his way, and if he could possibly swing it, he was going to be sure that we all joined him in his folly. He was demonstrating one of the traits of a fool that is easy to copy when you live or work in close proximity to that kind of behavior on an ongoing basis. It is easy to become childish.

Some of the characteristics of fools are similar to those of adolescents who are stubbornly determined that they will rule the world no matter the consequences. As any parent knows, the worst thing you can do is to become like your child when that sort of thing is going on. If you do, then every discussion becomes a spat between two children.

The same thing is true with your fool. When you interact with a fool, the very last stance you need to take with him or her is that of a child. If you do, to put it in plain language, "He will chew you up and spit you out." Your childish response will be thrown right back on you. You just can't afford to be anything but mature and wise when you are responding to your fool. Consequently, it is important for you to recognize the marks of childishness and learn what to do about them.

PUTTING AWAY CHILDISH THINGS

The apostle Paul had to deal with his share of fools; we can see by his writings that he came up against them all the time. But he also had to deal with the childish people, people like you and me, who longed to grow beyond where they were. In 1 Corinthians 13:11, Paul wrote almost wistfully and pleadingly, "When I was a child, I used to speak as a child, think as a child, reason as a child; when I became a man [an adult, *a mature person*], I did away with childish things" (NASB).

Do you need to "do away with"—let go of—some childish behavior that keeps popping up in your life? Paul said three things are

characteristic of children, and these are the cha~~~
let go: *speaking* like children, *reasoning* like chil~
children. If you find yourself having any of the
to your fool, then this is an area where you can g~~~

How Do Children Speak?

Proverbs 17:28 says, "Even a fool is thought wise if he keeps silent, and discerning if he holds his tongue." *The biggest attorney in Atlanta* never thought how foolish he looked when he decided to make his demanding little speech in the gate area. For all I know, he may have been a fool acting like a fool, or he may have been a frustrated man acting like a fool. He had his brief moment in the sun, and that probably is all I and the other people in the gate area that day will ever know of him. I don't have to deal with him on a daily basis. If I did, I'd need a lot of wisdom in order to keep from becoming equally childish in my responses, blurting out words that should not be said.

Children can sometimes be embarrassing because they blurt out *whatever* they think *whenever* they think it *to whomever* they wish without considering what effect their words have on anyone else. Childish speech doesn't consider the consequences. Now, for a child to speak like a child is expected, but for an adult to speak like a child throws everyone within earshot off balance. It is embarrassing and disconcerting.

What is childish speech for an adult? Well, if we were to categorize a roomful of adults according to their communication style when they were displeased with some circumstance or someone's behavior, we'd probably end up with one group of "shouters" and one group of "pouters." We would find all varieties of intensity and all forms of justification across the spectrum, but the thing that would make both styles equally foolish is the fact that neither group takes consequences into account.

shouter says, "Well, I just had to say it. It was on the tip of my ongue, and before I knew it, it had come out; I just couldn't help myself." After a few minutes of silence, while all those within range pick verbal buckshot out of their emotions, the shouter usually pipes up with, "Well, I had to get it off my chest; now *I* feel better." Shouters have put in their two cents' worth, but the people who are exposed to their childish style of communication have to put up protective barriers—barriers that block relationships and consequently hurt both the shouters and their "victims."

An equally expressive group of communicators usually feels very virtuous whenever a shouter pops off. They think, *I would never say anything like that! I would never speak in such an uncivil way!* It's true they may not respond as loudly or in such a quickly noticeable way as the shouters. But they do respond in a childish, manipulative way. When they perceive that they have been wronged, they may not speak at all for three days, righteously believing, by golly, that they would *never* be uncivil in expressing their displeasure! Yet the impact of a pouter's silence can be as damaging as a shouter's outbursts. A pouter's insides are eaten up by the venom bubbling beneath the surface, and there is no denying that everyone in the vicinity will eventually know it. The pouter just won't use words. She will frost the atmosphere with her body language and seething silence. Like the shouters, pouters fail to take into consideration that their behavior has grave consequences in their relationships.

What's *your* communication style? It may be that because you have been so caught up in what your fool is doing, you haven't looked at your own way of communicating. You may have imitated your fool's style without even being aware of it.

That's what happened to Delores. She found herself clamming up whenever Karl pulled one of his silent tantrums. If he decided to punish her with his withering silence (which could last for weeks), then Delores would do the same. Instead of maintaining her integrity as an individual and being true to who she was as a Christian, Delores became Karl's clone. She thought there was no other way to be. If Karl was silent and punishing, then she had to be silent and punishing right back. Needless to say, Karl and Delores's children received a powerful message: If Dad is mad, Mom is mad; and no one else exists until one of them gets over being mad! Delores needs to wise up and realize that just because Karl doesn't communicate, that is no reason for her to fall into his pattern. She is free to continue being who she is, saying what she wants to say. If Karl doesn't respond, so be it.

When by either shouting or pouting you become like the person who is mistreating you, you hand over the controls to him. You say, in so many words, "It's okay for you to shout [or pout] and for you to make me shout [or pout]. I have no control over my own emotions or reactions."

Some fools shout, and some pout. That is their choice; but *you* have choices as well. If you want to respond maturely and be a person of wisdom, you can't react in either way. If you speak like a child, you will shout or pout your way right into the vortex of anger and chaos that surrounds your fool. You will propel yourself into the middle of the problem and become what you never thought you would be: an angry, shouting, pouting person! You don't have to do it, so don't!

One of the characteristics of being an adult is having an awareness that the words you speak impact others. When you become an adult, you notice the power of the words you choose and the way you choose to speak them. When you become an adult, childish speech is inappropriate, and you are aware of it—sufficiently aware so that you choose to stop it. Even if you are comfortable with it, because it's how you've always talked when the pressure is on, you make the choice to "do away with" that kind of speech. As difficult as it is to believe, it is truly that easy. Just do away with it; put it away. Putting it away is your way of controlling your own inappropriate and childish reactions. Putting it away is resisting the urge to engage in verbal battle with a fool. You could do it, but it is of no use. You will never win.

Wanda learned to put away her childish speech as she interacted with her beloved fool, her husband, Marvin. Wanda had been raised in a family of six girls whose parents always spoke freely and sometimes very argumentatively. As the girls grew, they became women who could argue with the best of them—and they did.

Marvin was a match for Wanda, however, because he turned out to be an angry fool who used his silence as a weapon. It drove Wanda to absolute distraction when her husband became quiet and sullen. To provoke him to communicate, Wanda would don her best childhood tactics and badger Marvin until he blew up. They would have awful brawls, and after they were over, Wanda would feel terrible. Her children were devastated by the fights, and Marvin would immediately retreat to his gray-lipped silence once he'd exploded. Nothing constructive was ever accomplished through this couple's childish interaction.

It finally occurred to Wanda that she could do nothing to change Marvin's angry communication, but she could certainly refrain from being involved in it. She did not have to stay on his level and continue participating in his abusive episodes. She saw that she was allowing Marvin to define who she was as she reacted to everything he did, especially his punishing silences. She recognized that her own reactions were childish, that engaging in verbal badgering only caused damage to her and her children. She didn't want to be controlled by her fool any longer, and so she determined that she would put away her reactionary speech.

Wanda found out she really did have a choice about how she interacted with her fool. She determined to "set a guard" over her mouth (Psalm 141:3), to count to ten before she considered loosing her tongue when her husband was pushing her buttons, and to behave like a woman of dignity instead of like a demanding child. As a result of Wanda's decision to put away her childish behavior, the atmosphere in her home became much more peaceful. Marvin still retreated into his punishing silences, but they no longer worked on his wife. Wanda went about her business, refusing to engage her husband when he was behaving manipulatively. No more badgering, no more blowups, no more crying children. Wanda had wised up.

How Do Children Think and Reason?

The other marks of childishness mentioned by Paul are *thinking* and *reasoning* like a child. The obvious question to ask is, How do children think and reason? It doesn't take long to answer that. We all know children, and as dear as they may be to us, the truth is they think about themselves and what they can get for themselves. Then they reason, if ever so guilelessly, how they can get what they want. Wherever there are children, there is a little squabble waiting to break out or little feelings waiting to get hurt, because they want what they want when they want it.

If you are focusing on your fool, expecting him to give you what you want, then you are engaging in childish thinking. When you link up with a fool, you'll find that there is very little thought for you. A fool is so absorbed with himself that his giving is usually self-serving: He gives in order to get. If you think and reason like a child as you try to "squeeze blood from a turnip," you'll be very disappointed.

Just ask Lindy, an immature woman who is struggling to grow up. In her immaturity, she has sought out people to fulfill her wants and heal her pains. Her first marriage ended when she convinced herself that Joe just couldn't meet her needs. She hated his emotional distancing and silence and couldn't bear the idea that someone would ignore her when she cried.

Shortly into her second marriage she found that her expectations of Tad also were far beyond his willingness to fulfill. Tad is a fool who is easy to love when he is winning people into his confidence. Lindy was like a fly looking for a place to land, and Tad's web was convenient. But within three months, Lindy discovered that Tad was not going to care for her as she wanted to be cared for, and he was not going to make her first in his life. He couldn't, because *he* is first. He is the center of his universe, and the only reasons he gave Lindy the time of day were because she looked good on his arm and he thought she'd be fun to have around. It didn't take long for both of them to reason, *You are not what I want. You don't make me feel important.*

In a moment of profound sadness, Lindy looked in the mirror and saw a woman who had failed at one marriage and was headed for a repeat performance in this one. She could not believe that she was no closer to fulfilling her hopes and dreams at this point in her life. She knew she was stuck in a situation that would require wisdom that she had never bothered to appropriate.

As she looked at the mascara mingled with the tears running down her face, Lindy determined, *It's time to grow up!* She did not have to have Tad's acceptance to be a whole person. She could be whole with or without his attention or approval. She had been told this by several friends who had seen her pitiful choices, but she hadn't been ready to embrace the truth about her immature thinking and childish behavior. During that sad, enlightening moment in front of the mirror, Lindy finally became willing to put away her childish thinking about what she just *had to have* from her husband.

Things changed quickly for Tad and Lindy. She left her childlike neediness behind and made it clear to Tad that he was free to stay in the marriage or leave it. She said she had no plans to leave, but she would no longer hold on to Tad by her childish clinging. As a result of Lindy's new strength, Tad came face to face with his powerful need to be in control. He was already convinced that he didn't really want Lindy, but he certainly didn't like the reality that she was perfectly capable of living with or without him.

After several months of living off balance in their new relational dynamic, Tad and Lindy are still plugging away at learning about how to have an adult-to-adult relationship. Their marriage may or may not survive, but Lindy knows *she* will. She has become a mature woman who is no longer controlled by her own immature thinking or by the fool in her life.

BREAKING THE CYCLE

Consider your relationship with your fool. Are there areas in your life where you are still holding out to get what you want from him or her? Are you continuing to invest energy into getting your fool to do what you want? Is there anything you have determined to accomplish in his or her life? Have you been working on your fool for the past twenty-five years? Are you determined that one of you will change or one of you will die? Are you holding on to a set of impossible expectations because *that is what you want?*

As you begin to mature in relating to your fool, you will learn to put those thoughts and strategies aside. You will consciously let them go— no matter how badly you want to hold on to them. It is a childish dream to believe your fool will become the person you want him to be. It is an immature hope that through what you say or do or try to make happen, your fool will one day turn around and say, "You know, you are right. I have been wrong. I'm sorry."

It takes maturity to lay aside the childish schemes we use to control the important people in our lives. It takes real wisdom to become whole, functional people who are aware of the childish thoughts and behaviors that have buoyed us up in our struggle with our fools. It takes courage to admit that they do us no good and that we do them no good. Rather, they keep us stuck in a place where there is no air and no hope.

Are you ready, my friend, to lay your childishness aside and accept your situation for what it is? Just like putting away the clothes that no longer fit you after junior high and replacing them with more appropriate attire, you have to put away some old behaviors if you want to break the cycle of foolish reactions and results. They don't fit you anymore and are not appropriate for the new life you are going to lead.

It's time to "put on some new clothes"—to look toward the future and discover ways to act out of the wiser, more mature you. Soon you will find that you are more comfortable in your new "look." You will be more at ease with yourself and more comfortable in your position with God. And, to your great relief, your fool will be less and less the focus of your life.

Let's move on and look through your new wardrobe. You have a lot to look forward to!

Putting away childish thinking and childish behavior is a challenge, but it is one of the healthiest things you can do for yourself as well as for everyone with whom you interact. It's easy to maintain childishness as a weapon against your fool and fail to realize how your immature thinking and behavior holds people you care about at arm's length. Unpredictability, volatility, demanding what you want when you want it (even if you don't get it!)—all are characteristics of childishness that can be put away with a determined effort on your part.

Think About It

1. It's time for a little personal assessment. Make a list of the ways you speak like a child.

2. Now make a list of the ways you think and reason like a child.

3. In what specific ways has your childish speech or reasoning added to the chaos of the situation with your fool?

4. Can you see how it would be possible to "do away with" this behavior? If so, how? If not, why not?

Go to God About It

Anytime we set out to change our thinking or our behavior, it is a lost cause unless we are fully aware that apart from God's power in our lives we will fail in the long run. Oh, we can clean up our acts for a while, but it takes a deep inner transformation for our thinking and behavior to change permanently.

Note in the passage below who begins the work of transformation in you.

Philippians 1:3-6

I thank my God every time I remember you. In all my prayers for all of you, I always pray with joy because of your partnership in the gospel from the first day until now, being confident of this, that he who began a good work in you will carry it on to completion until the day of Christ Jesus.

If you have believed the gospel, confessed and repented of your sins, and determined to head in another direction, then God promises to keep you going on the path of righteousness. But you must make sure that you have given him a place to begin his work in you.

We all begin at the same place by recognizing that we can't live life on our own. We are in desperate need of a Savior. Romans 3:23 says,

"For all have sinned and fall short of the glory of God." We all have fallen short of the mark that God has set as acceptable to him. Because of our human nature, we can never reach it. "For the wages of sin is death" (Romans 6:23). That's the bad news. But there is good news! The rest of the verse promises, "but the gift of God is eternal life in Christ Jesus our Lord."

God didn't set the mark impossibly high so we would fail; he set it there so that he could remain perfectly holy and righteous. To lower it would mean that his standard is negotiable and anything goes. Instead of compromising himself, God loved us enough to leave his heavenly domain, come to earth in Christ, and take our deserved punishment on his absolutely sinless body. He died so that we could live. "But God demonstrates his own love for us in this: While we were still sinners, Christ died for us" (Romans 5:8).

Consult the Bible About It

It's probably been awhile since you looked at what your salvation cost Jesus (God in the flesh). Or perhaps you've never recognized what Jesus did for you and how much you need the salvation he offers. Take some time to carefully read through the passage below, noting how expensive your life was to purchase.

Philippians 2:5-16
Your attitude should be the same as that of Christ Jesus:

Who, being in very nature God,
    did not consider equality with God something to be
        grasped,

but made himself nothing,
taking the very nature of a servant,
being made in human likeness.
And being found in appearance as a man,
he humbled himself
and became obedient to death—
even death on a cross!
Therefore God exalted him to the highest place
and gave him the name that is above every name,
that at the name of Jesus every knee should bow,
in heaven and on earth and under the earth,
and every tongue confess that Jesus Christ is Lord,
to the glory of God the Father.

Therefore, my dear friends, as you have always obeyed—not only in my presence, but now much more in my absence—continue to work out your salvation with fear and trembling, for it is God who works in you to will and to act according to his good purpose.

Do everything without complaining or arguing, so that you may become blameless and pure, children of God without fault in a crooked and depraved generation, in which you shine like stars in the universe as you hold out the word of life—in order that I may boast on the day of Christ that I did not run or labor for nothing.

1. What did your life cost Christ?

2. What did Christ gain through his death?

3. Now, what is your challenge?

What Will You Do About It?

If you believe that you need a Savior and that apart from Christ living in you, you are bound to fail at your effort to put away childish things, then perhaps this is a good time for you to make a simple exchange: his life for yours! Christ died that you might live, and that is the wonderful offer he extends to you. Your job? Receive what he offers. John 1:12 promises, "Yet to all who received him, to those who believed in his name, he gave the right to become children of God."

If you would like to respond to God's offer of salvation (spiritual wholeness), then you can exchange your life for his, knowing that this is the only way you can approach a holy God. You can't "make the grade," but God in Christ did that for you on the cross. The Bible says he was not only just but he was our justifier (see Romans 3:26). Picture it: You're standing before a judge who bangs the gavel and declares you "guilty." Then he stands, removes his robes of justice, and comes down from his bench to tell you, "You are guilty, but I will take your punishment for you." You didn't receive what you deserved. The judge has given you mercy. And that's what the gift of salvation is all about: a God who became a man and died for you, because you deserved death and would perish without his intervention!

If you admit that you are guilty and you would like to receive the eternal gift of God by giving all you know of you to all you know of him, then why not write out a simple prayer telling God that is what you want to do. Be sure to date it so you have a permanent record of the day you exchanged your life for the life of Jesus Christ.

John 8:34-36

Jesus replied, "I tell you the truth, everyone who sins is a slave to sin. Now a slave has no permanent place in the family, but a son belongs to it forever. So if the Son sets you free, you will be free indeed.

Hallelujah! And welcome to the family!

Trust in the LORD with all your heart
and lean not on your own understanding;
in all your ways acknowledge him,
and he will make your paths straight.

PROVERBS 3:5-6

However confused the scene of our life appears,
however torn we may be who now do face that scene,
it may be faced, and we can go on to be whole.

RUKEYSER

Save us from hotheads that would lead us to act foolishly
and from cold feet that would keep us from acting at all.

SENATE PRAYERS

If God sends us on stony paths,
he provides strong shoes.

CORRIE TEN BOOM

CHAPTER NINE

New Strategies for Old Battles

So how does a wise person think and behave in response to a fool? What can you do differently to begin to extricate yourself from the chaos, control, and despair that bind you in a painful and unhealthy dynamic?

I have learned that anytime I start asking myself, *What am I going to do?* I have one safe place to go. James 1:5 advises me, "If any of you lacks wisdom, let him ask of God" (NASB). That can sound pat, but it really isn't; it is profound. When you ask God for wisdom, you are admitting, *I am out of wisdom myself. My supply is exhausted. I cannot reason my way out of this one.* In the great scheme of things, this is the most wonderful place you can be. This is when God shines brightest in your life. When the background of the situation is the blackest, the diamond of God's wisdom sparkles clearest.

Once you determine to admit that you have no wisdom of your own and you are willing to quit saying, "But, God..." and start humbly confessing that you don't know what to do, he *promises* to give you wisdom. Proverbs 2:2-5 (NASB) says:

Make your ear attentive to wisdom,
Incline your heart to understanding;

For if you cry for discernment,

Lift your voice for understanding;

If you seek her as silver,

And search for her as for hidden treasures;

Then you *will* discern the fear of the LORD,

And discover the knowledge of God.

God's wisdom has a particular set of characteristics. James 3:17-18 describes those characteristics this way: "But the wisdom from above is first pure, then peaceable, gentle, reasonable, full of mercy and good fruits, unwavering, without hypocrisy. And the seed whose fruit is right-eousness is sown in peace by those who make peace" (NASB).

William Barclay, in *The Daily Study Bible* (St. Andrew Press, 1958), provides insight into these characteristics. When wisdom is *pure*, Barclay explained, it is "cleansed of all ulterior motive." It won't be devious, always looking for a way to glorify self. When it is *peaceable*, it will "produce right relationships," if possible. That isn't always possible, but when wisdom is in charge, at least there is potential for healthy relating. When it is *reasonable*, wisdom "gives a man the right to forgive when strict justice gives him the perfect right to condemn." You may have biblical permission to hold on to "strict justice," but if you do, you erect another barrier to what God, in his mercy, might do in the situation. When wisdom is *gentle*, it is "willing to listen, willing to be persuaded, skilled in knowing when to wisely yield" and when to wisely stand firm. When it is *full of mercy and good fruits,* it will "offer mercy to any man who is in trouble, even if he has brought that trouble on himself." (Even if he is a fool!) "We can never say we have truly pitied anyone until we have helped him." But we must have the wisdom to understand what true help really is. No doubt, you have tried to help your fool, but if help is not motivated by godly wisdom, it can be deadly. When wisdom is *unwavering*, it is "not hesitant and vacillating; it means that it knows its own mind, chooses its own course, and abides by it," Barclay wrote. And, he added, wisdom *without hypocrisy* "never deals in deception for its own ends. It is not the wisdom that is clever at putting on disguises and concealing its real aims and motives."

Note that the goal of seeking wisdom is not making your fool into a better person but rather making you into a healthy, fully functioning, godly person. If you seek wisdom, you will "discern the fear of the LORD, and discover the knowledge of God" (Proverbs 2:5, NASB). That's what it's all about. That will stabilize you and affirm you in the stand you take. Your action will not be a knee-jerk response to your fool and his folly but a controlled, intelligent response based on the wisdom God gives you.

I believe I witnessed a woman of wisdom in action just last week. It was Friday night at Wal-Mart, the gathering spot for the gene pool of America. I spotted a man in his seventies accompanied by an elegantly dressed woman. He was talking in a very loud voice that everyone within three aisles either direction could hear. When I saw the commotion, I inched my way to where he was, thinking to myself, *This is going to be a good one*. And sure enough, I wasn't disappointed.

Waving his hands and hollering in his most abrasive, intimidating tone, the elderly customer was accusing the checkout clerk of cheating him. He insisted that the electronic scanner was set at too fast a clip, but the truth was that he simply couldn't keep up. In big-mouthed-fool fashion, he demanded a rescan of all of his purchases.

His wife, who had been standing next to him, quietly slipped into the crowd in the front of the store. No doubt, she had experienced her husband's foolish behavior before. It was obvious that he really didn't

...d his outburst or what they thought, and embarrassing his
...as of no concern to him. As I watched this couple, I could see that
his wife had learned how to put space between herself and her fool as he
exposed his folly to everyone within earshot. She neither shouted nor
pouted; she just knew she needed to step back and get out of his way. A
woman of lesser wisdom would have tried to rescue him from his situation or would have taken him on with an argument. This woman did
neither. She laid down whatever words were on the tip of her tongue and
let her husband go his foolish way. She did not have to be part of the
crazy scene, and she was mature enough to know it!

Because fools are angry people, prone to childish shouting or pouting to express their hostility, it's important to respond to their anger in
an adult manner. When a fool erupts, you need to recognize that the
anger being thrown at you is intended to bring about a response. It is
designed to make you sad, to make you behave, to make you fearful, or
to push you away. If you respond predictably, that anger will be used on
you again to elicit your predictable response. If you respond with tears
every time, you are predictable. If you withdraw, you are predictable. If
you apologize and promise to do better, you are predictable. If you leave,
you are predictable. If you fight back, you are predictable.

The Scriptures say, "An angry man stirs up dissension, and a hot-
tempered one commits many sins" (Proverbs 29:22). The New American
Standard Bible translates it this way: "An angry man stirs up strife, and a
hot-tempered man abounds in transgression." Since this is the case, if you
intend to be a wise person when you face your angry person, you need to
think carefully before you react. "A simple man believes anything, but
a prudent man gives thought to his steps," advises Proverbs 14:15. If
you want to be wise, your focus has to be on you and what you can do

differently in relationship with your fool. Rather than being a victim or a martyr, or rather than being equally angry and foolish in your automatic responses, you can try something new.

TURN AWAY FROM EVIL

Turning away from the evil of the angry person is the only way to effectively deal with your fool when he is angry or irrational. You may not always go away physically, but because you are in control of "you," you can turn away emotionally. Instead of reasoning (again) that this time you can win over your fool and avoid his wrath, you can use a whole different approach.

Try this exercise the next time you are confronted with your fool's anger. Imagine yourself in a castle. Around any self-respecting castle there is a moat. In this moat there are dangerous creatures. Across this moat there is a drawbridge, and whoever dwells inside the castle has control of the bridge.

When you see your angry fool approaching, determine that you will not respond in the usual way. Instead resolve to quietly turn away by cranking up the drawbridge and saying to yourself, *I am turning away. My fool will not get to me.*

Because you have emotionally turned away, the usual angry outbursts will not have the same effect. Because your response will be different, you will not be under the control of your fool. You will be in control of what you do because you are *considering* your steps. You are being wise when you remember what the Scriptures say: "A gentle answer turns away wrath, but a harsh word stirs up anger" (Proverbs 15:1). You can calmly say, "I can't talk with you until you are less angry," just as well as you can scream it. You don't shrink from the truth, but you disengage your fool's power to control your response. If you purposely change your response, it will require some kind of change on the part of your fool. That is not to say the anger will stop, but you will no longer be allowing your fool to determine *your* reactions. You will be taking responsibility for yourself.

It is possible to have peace even when your fool is on a rampage. Proverbs 18:10 says, "The name of the LORD is a strong tower; the righteous runs into it and is safe" (NASB). If you want to be safe with the Lord and free of the chaos and insanity that combat with your fool inevitably brings, you will have to choose to run to a safe place. Earlier I referred to it as a castle. You may want to call it a strong tower. The point is to recognize that it is God himself who is your ultimate protection. The name of the Lord is where you run, because it is there you can find a safety and a peace that are beyond you.

The name of the Lord represents all that he is to you. If you need peace, he is the Prince of Peace; if you need counsel, he is the Wonderful Counselor; if you need a God who will be in control, he is the Mighty God. Because he is whatever you need, you can know that you will be protected even when your fool is acting his part. Your emotional and spiritual well-being are protected within the walls of the castle. This concept works whether you are dealing with someone you see casually or regularly. Just try it. It has worked for many people in diverse situations.

Lest I be misunderstood, I must make one thing very clear: If you are in physical danger, no imaginary castle or drawbridge will protect you. If you have been hit or threatened, then you have only one choice: to leave the physical presence of the person who is threatening you. Violent anger can be dealt with only from afar and with the help of the law.

A young bride was recently devastated when her husband of two months severely bruised her by throwing her against a wall. She wisely called the police, and they took her husband to jail for a night. When he saw her two days later and she showed him her bruises, he said, "I can't believe I had to go to jail for *that!*" Fools never see what they do as harmful because their reality is *their* reality. Truth is whatever they make it out to be; therefore, whatever they do is acceptable in their own eyes. When fools become violent, wise people get out of their way!

OVERCOME EVIL WITH GOOD

Because a fool scoffs at wisdom, rejects all counsel, and refuses to humble himself and change, you may never succeed in bringing peace to your relationship with your fool. God knows that, and that's why his Word says, "*If possible, so far as it depends on you,* be at peace with all men" (Romans 12:18, NASB, emphasis added). It is obvious that it may not be possible to be at peace with your fool, but there are some basic rules that apply in every situation. Paul summed them up in his instructions on how to treat an enemy:

> Never pay back evil for evil to anyone. Respect what is right in the sight of all men. If possible, so far as it depends on you, be at peace with all men. Never take your own revenge, beloved, but leave room for the wrath of God, for it is written, "Vengeance is Mine, I will repay," says the LORD. "But if your enemy is hungry, feed him, and if he is thirsty, give him a drink; for in so doing you will heap burning coals upon his head." Do not be overcome by evil, but overcome evil with good. (Romans 12:17-21, NASB)

Basically, God says that as we do what is best for our fool we supply his needs—and in doing so we may be pointing out his folly. In biblical times "coals" were a common source of heat, so people had a desperate need if their coals grew cold and died. When they needed live coals, they would go to their neighbor to get them and then carry them home in a large pan on top of their heads. A real need was met.

That is what you are to do for your fool. Being kind to him doesn't mean giving in to his manipulation and demands and responding with "good stuff." When you understand that the fool's most desperate need is to wise up, then your generous kindness becomes a strategy to point out his folly. By your goodness you will paint a contrast that maybe even your fool can "get." And whether or not your fool "gets it," you will have done the right thing. Your goal in relating to your fool will be to overcome his evil by doing good for the purpose of exposing his folly and bringing the fool to repentance.

"Doing good" to someone who repeatedly hurts you can seem a bitter pill to swallow. But the wisdom from above never shouts, "An eye for an eye!" Rather, Scripture says,

> Who is wise and understanding among you? Let him show it by his good life, by deeds done in the humility that comes from wisdom. But if you harbor bitter envy and selfish ambition in your hearts, do not boast about it or deny the truth. Such "wisdom" does not come down from heaven but is earthly, unspiritual, of the devil. For where you have envy and selfish ambition, there you find disorder and every evil practice. (James 3:13-16)

Overcoming evil with good can be a daunting task if you are harboring bitterness in your heart. The most effective thing you can do to rid yourself of bitterness is to make the choice to forgive your fool. The dictionary says to forgive means "to send away your right to punish," "to send away the offense," or "to release the one who has offended you from any obligation." If your fool can't or won't make peace with you, you can still forgive him. As you forgive your fool and treat him with the respect you would accord a stranger, you will see the dynamic between you change. You may find that it is still not possible to be at peace, but you will have provided the atmosphere for peace to reign on your side of the street. By forgiving, you will be better off.

DETACH

When you're not sure exactly how to proceed in relating to your fool, the best thing you can do is to "detach." The best way I know to describe detaching is that you begin to treat your fool as a stranger. Now, I'm not talking about the kind of stranger with whom you make no eye contact and have no conversation. I'm talking about the kind of stranger you encounter as a waiter or a sales associate in the store or as the office manager at your doctor's office. When you encounter one of these people, you are probably polite, kind, and share only the information that needs to be given in order to conduct the business you have. When you detach from your fool, he becomes this kind of "stranger" to you. You do not open yourself up for intimate conversation about either of you, but you do speak with civility and kindness.

I have observed some remarkable results with ex-spouses who begin to treat their former mates as strangers. In their determination to be civil, kind, nonrevealing, and noninvasive, a new relationship is formed. Things don't always go smoothly, but for the most part the communication improves when at least one party sets aside weapons and strategies that belonged to past conflicts. If you determine that you will not become engaged in combat, then you can have more control over the tenor of the conversation and the atmosphere of the interaction.

Remember Sharon from chapter seven—the woman who couldn't stand the angry person she was becoming as she thrashed around in relating to her ex-husband? Well, she finally determined that her former husband, Chris, would become as a stranger to her. She would treat him as she would treat anyone she met casually. She would be polite and exchange pleasantries, but she staunchly refused to be drawn into a quarrel. Whenever she had to deal with him on any subject, she prepared ahead of time by pulling up her imaginary drawbridge. She began to spend time in prayer instead of in combat. Chris didn't change, but she did. She found peace and a sense of rightness in the whole of her life. No longer was she allowing her fool to define her, nor was she being drawn into angry behavior that was not becoming of the Christian woman she claimed to be.

At a conference recently where I was speaking on "Foolproofing Your Life," I had just described this new way of interacting when a woman in the back of the room raised her hand and said, "You know, in Kentucky there's a saying about that kind of thing."

I smiled as I thought of the wonderful folk wisdom of the hills. "What is that?" I asked.

She said, "That's when you feed someone with a long-handled spoon!"

I had to laugh as I thought of how hard I had struggled to draw a picture of detaching, of treating someone as a stranger, and here it was in a tidy package. Next time you feel yourself getting sucked into an emotional "food fight" with your crazy-making fool, try feeding him with a long-handled spoon!

SPEAK THE TRUTH

Let's say you've run into your castle and you've chosen to pull up the drawbridge. You are trusting God to be everything you need and to give you wisdom in responding to your fool. You are making a conscious decision to exclude the influence of your fool from your emotions, but still things happen that bring anger to your heart. What do you do at this point? Is there a legitimate time to be angry, and is there ever a useful purpose for anger?

Proverbs 19:11 says, "A man's wisdom gives him patience; it is to his glory to overlook an offense." It is apparent that being slow to anger is the best thing you can do. When you relate to a fool on a regular basis, it's easy to become touchy. That's understandable. Anything that is picked at constantly will fester and become raw. Dealing with a fool can be such an infuriating experience that you become very sensitive to every foolish word he utters, sometimes even to things that are harmless.

If you're in this situation, Proverbs 17:14 gives you specific advice: "The beginning of strife is like letting out water, so abandon the quarrel before it breaks out" (NASB). In other words, it is to your advantage to turn away from a fight before it happens, because once the first word has been spoken, it is like letting out water: It is impossible to stop it. This is where you learn that wise principle of "choosing" your battles. Some things just aren't worth squabbling over; they only muddy the water and keep you embroiled and off balance.

But what if you are legitimately angry, and you must do something about it? What if you have a situation with your fool that is so vexing it must be handled directly? God knows and understands that sometimes you have a very legitimate reason to be angry. That's what I love about our God: He walked among us, and he was angry over the injustices that fools caused people to suffer. If you doubt that, just check out what he had to say to the Pharisees—religious fools who thought they were always right and who didn't care who got hurt! His harsh words in Matthew 23:33 are just one example: "You snakes! You brood of vipers! How will you escape being condemned to hell?"

When you are angry, however, I recommend following the advice Paul gave in Ephesians 4:25-27: "Therefore each of you must put off falsehood and speak truthfully to his neighbor, for we are all members of one body. 'In your anger do not sin': Do not let the sun go down while you are still angry, and do not give the devil a foothold." If you don't want to be like your fool, then you must make a conscious choice to go another direction. You must "speak the truth" with strength and dignity. In doing so, you are assuming responsibility and not leaving it up to your fool to define you or your relationship with him.

Knowing that one of the major marks of a fool is his unwillingness to look at the facts, you may ask, "What good will it do to speak the truth if it is just going to be thrown in my face?" Think about it, my friend: Maybe you need to speak the truth for *you*. Maybe you need to hear yourself calmly saying what is true instead of arguing and using angry words as weapons to defend yourself or wound your fool. It is important to speak the truth, even if only one of you is listening. When you simply speak the truth and then refuse to be drawn into combat, your wisdom will lead you to safety. Your fool may still be angry, but you will not be battered by useless battle. You will find the inner clarity you need to disengage, back away, go to your castle, and begin to pray, simply asking God what to do next.

PRAY

Just as you must admit that you need divine wisdom, it is important to acknowledge that you don't know how to pray—especially for your fool. No doubt, if you love your fool, you have spent a lot of time asking God to change him, to change the circumstances, to remove whatever is causing your fool to be so foolish. If you've taken quite an emotional beating and your love has run dry, you may even have resorted to crying, "Lord, just do away with him!" Either way has you focusing on your fool again.

So how can you pray in a way that makes a difference? Praying is similar to having wisdom—the whole direction must come from God. Effective prayer does not originate with you, nor is it something magic you can drum up by using just the "right" words. Romans 8:26-27 tells us, "In the same way, the Spirit helps us in our weakness. We do not know what we ought to pray for, but the Spirit himself intercedes for us with groans that words cannot express. And he who searches our hearts knows the mind of the Spirit, because the Spirit intercedes for the saints in accordance with God's will."

We are told that we don't know how to pray as we should. So when you pray for your fool and your situation, confess that right up front. Opening up your dialogue with God with the simple sentence, "I don't know how to pray as I should," can roll a heavy burden off your shoulders. You don't have to think up what to pray or how to say it. You don't have to rummage through the right prayer book to find the perfect prayer. All you have to do is confess that you are totally clueless as to how to pray, and then God promises that the Spirit himself will pray through you with groanings that can't be uttered. To those who are related to him, God promises help in their helplessness.

NTANGLING the TIGHTEST KNOTS

be thinking, This is all great stuff, Jan, but you don't know what it's like in my world. You don't live in my house or deal with my fool. I can't just "detach" and move on with my life. It's not that simple!

I hear you. Sometimes the strings that tie you to your fool are knotted so tightly you feel like there's no way to get disentangled. After all, you may even be *married* to your beloved fool. How on earth do you manage to disengage from a spouse's control and remain married? If you have no biblical grounds to divorce, what are you to do? Your fool hasn't been unfaithful, nor has he abandoned you; in fact, he sticks closer to home than bubblegum on a shoe!

This is not an uncommon problem, and it's one that begs for a great deal of wisdom and understanding. As I see it, for a Christian who's married to a fool, there are two options in the eyes of God. One is to remain married and to respond to the fool with a gentle, quiet spirit. For example, the apostle Peter offered advice to the woman whose husband is disobedient to the Word of God. A fool would qualify here.

> Wives, in the same way be submissive to your husbands so that,
> if any of them do not believe the word, they may be won over
> without words by the behavior of their wives, when they see the
> purity and reverence of your lives. Your beauty should not come
> from outward adornment, such as braided hair and the wearing
> of gold jewelry and fine clothes. Instead, it should be that of
> your inner self, the unfading beauty of a gentle and quiet spirit,
> which is of great worth in God's sight. For this is the way the
> holy women of the past who put their hope in God used to
> make themselves beautiful. (1 Peter 3:1-5)

I believe the spirit of Peter's advice (to live obediently to and in dependence on God) also applies to husbands married to foolish wives. If a husband or wife can tolerate living with a strife-filled mate, then that is what he or she needs to do, while maintaining an inner peace that hopes in God. If the strength or the inclination to do that just isn't there, the apostle Paul offers additional advice in 1 Corinthians 7:10-11: "To the married I give this command (not I, but the Lord): A wife must not separate from her husband. But if she does, she must remain unmarried or else be reconciled to her husband." (Again, I believe Paul's teaching applies equally to husbands.)

If your spouse's anger and strife are too much for you to bear and you do not feel you can continue to put up with the situation, you are free to separate from your spouse. From that point on, your option is either to reconcile with him or her or to remain unmarried. By reconciliation I do not mean going back for "more of the same" after a break from one another. Biblical reconciliation requires brokenness and humility within each individual, and that rarely comes quickly. The person who reconciles must be prepared by God to fit together with a mate who has been prepared by God as well.

You may believe that true reconciliation is out of reach, and if you are married to a fool, you may be right. But don't discount what God can do in a fool's heart and mind when he or she is stripped of all the comforts of having a spouse! Until a fool is left by a mate seeking a saner and wiser way, why should he change in order to live at peace in the relationship? Granted, your spouse may cry "foul" and divorce you if you leave. If that happens, then your options change; but for the time being, if you find that you cannot live with your fool, God frees you to live without him and remain unmarried.

This final caveat, "remain unmarried," is a good test for you person-ally. Are you willing to face the fact that your mate may not reconcile, may never marry anyone else, and may not die for a long time? Are you willing to live without a mate and still be content? I have found that this is a good personal litmus test for an individual bound to a fool through marriage when things are stressful and strife is at a high pitch. Ask yourself, *Am I willing to separate, remain unmarried, or be reconciled?* If not, then "detach-ment" is the option that will allow you to remain married, to hope in God, and to maintain a sense of peace in the midst of your circumstances.

The next obvious question is, But is that a marriage? The answer, of course, is no—not in the ideal sense. It is, however, a fulfillment of *your role and your* responsibility that you agreed to when you took your wedding vows. God has amazing ways of "showing up" when you make the often difficult choice to obey him, honor him, and allow him to determine the outcome of your situation without prescribing how you think he should fix things.

Tewannah is a woman who determined that she wanted to be in on what God was doing. She began to walk in obedience to him in every aspect of her life. While she said very little to her foolish husband, Jake, about what was going on in her life, he noticed changes he didn't like, and he refused to put up with them.

It wasn't long until something had to give. The strife was intense. Jake was even brandishing guns in an effort to make Tewannah act the way he wanted. She asked him to leave until they could find a point of reconciliation. He left, but he was determined there would be no recon-ciliation. He altered as much of his financial statement as he could to exclude Tewannah and their children, and then he divorced her.

Three years after all this family pain, Tewannah is quick to say, "I have never been cared for by the Lord in so many incredible ways. I wouldn't go back for anything in the world." Jake continues to give Tewannah as much grief as he can from afar, but she is a woman at peace whose God has been faithful in every imaginable way.

It is so very difficult to let go of one you have spent most of your life trying to make look better. It is hard to admit that you cannot satisfy someone you have tried repeatedly to please. It is defeating to realize you have no power to change your fool though you have tried to make things better and have worked overtime to appease. You have probably spent more than your fair share of time believing one of two lies: either "There has to be something more I can do" or "If only I were different, then everything would be okay."

I plead with you, my friend, to let go of those lies, to acknowledge that you don't have the power you've assumed you have. Arriving at this moment is tough; I know. It's a journey of a thousand hurts. It's a trip that sucks the life out of you, especially when you've believed you could always manage it. You could always find a way to roll with it, avoid it, or deny it. But no more. You are wising up and realizing that God has a better way for you.

How are you feeling now, my friend? Excited? Afraid? Unsure? The next step on the journey toward foolproofing your life can be a scary one, but it is the most liberating. Come along. It's time to surrender yourself and your beloved fool to the God who is all-wise, all-loving, all-powerful. He is the God of miracles, and he can be trusted!

There comes a time in most of our lives when we have nothing left to prove. We have given up the fantasy of being bigger and better than we really are in our chosen field or lifestyle, and we become content with what we have and who we are. For the person who deals with a fool on an ongoing basis, however, this kind of contentment is often very tenuous. If you love a fool, how can you find peace in the middle of the storm?

Our God gives wisdom and peace to those who genuinely pursue it. Are you ready to seriously consider, *What am I going to do now?* If so, God will show you some new strategies to use in your old battle with the fool in your life.

Think About It

"A man's wisdom gives him patience; it is to his glory to overlook an offense" (Proverbs 19:11). Isn't it interesting that "wisdom" gives us patience? I'm sure you've heard the admonition, "Don't pray for patience, because you'll get tribulation!" But let's face it: We already have tribulation. Hard times go along with being alive, but God uses those difficult times to make us better by giving us patience, experience, and hope (see Romans 5:3-5)! "And hope does not disappoint us, because God has poured out his love into our hearts by the Holy Spirit, whom he has given us" (Romans 5:5).

1. Think about a time recently when you needed patience. Be specific.

2. What were your thoughts in the middle of the situation?

3. How did you behave?

4. Did you behave the way you wanted to behave? Why or why not?

5. What do you consider to be your greatest weakness or need in dealing with difficult relationships?

Go to God About It

In this process of changing strategies, you must look to God for the wisdom you need, because there are no pat answers that apply to every case. Let's look at some Scripture verses that show you the heart of God and his willingness to give you what you need.

Read Paul's prayer for the Ephesian believers and then answer the questions that follow.

Ephesians 1:15-23

For this reason, ever since I heard about your faith in the Lord Jesus and your love for all the saints, I have not stopped giving thanks for you, remembering you in my prayers. I keep asking that the God of our Lord Jesus Christ, the glorious Father, may give you the Spirit of wisdom and revelation, so that you may know him better. I pray also that the eyes of your heart may be enlightened in order that you may know the hope to which he has called you, the riches of his glorious inheritance in the saints, and his incomparably great power for us who believe. That power is like the working of his mighty strength, which he exerted in Christ when he raised him from the dead and seated him at his right hand in the heavenly realms, far above all rule and authority, power and dominion, and every title that can be given, not only in the present age but also in the one to come. And God placed all things under his feet and appointed him to be head over everything for the church, which is his body, the fullness of him who fills everything in every way.

1. What specific things did Paul pray for these believers?

2. What kind of power did he pray would be operative in their lives?

3. Do you believe this power is available to you? Why or why not?

4. How might this power enable you to change your strategies for dealing with your fool?

Consult the Bible About It

Luke 8 tells one of my favorite faith-building stories in all of Scripture. Read it with your "stormy situation" in mind, and ask God what he would have you learn from the disciples' experience.

Luke 8:22-25

One day Jesus said to his disciples, "Let's go over to the other side of the lake." So they got into a boat and set out. As they sailed, he fell asleep. A squall came down on the lake, so that the boat was being swamped, and they were in great danger.

The disciples went and woke him, saying, "Master, Master, we're going to drown!"

He got up and rebuked the wind and the raging waters; the storm subsided, and all was calm. "Where is your faith?" he asked his disciples. In fear and amazement they asked one another, "Who is this? He commands even the winds and the water, and they obey him."

1. Who suggested the trip across the water?

2. What did the disciples deduce was going to happen to them?

3. To whom did they turn for help?

4. What did Jesus say to them?

5. What did the disciples learn through this stormy experience?

What Will You Do About It?

This could well be a time of deep struggle for you. If you are seriously considering changing your strategies, you have had to look at yourself and the ways you may have failed foolishly in the past. No one enjoys coming face to face with his own folly. When we become aware of the many times we have been wrong, it can be hard to take a stand for something we believe to be right.

Amy Carmichael, my favorite devotional author, is a woman who knew hard times, difficult people, and perplexing experiences. In her book *Candles in the Dark* (Christian Literature Crusade, 1982) we find these words to one of her students.

> I have a lovely word for you: Luke 4:30. "Jesus passing through the midst of them went His way." We are meant to pass through the midst of whatever comes and not get upset or even inwardly ruffled.
>
> A day or two ago I was thinking rather sadly of the past—

so many sins and failures and lapses of every kind. I was reading Isaiah 43, and in verse 24 I saw myself: "Thou hast wearied me with thine many iniquities." And then for the first time I noticed that there is no space between v. 24 and v. 25, "I, even I, am He that blotteth out thy transgressions for Mine own sake; and I will not remember thy sins." Who but our father would forgive like that?

So, my friend, no amount of past failure need stop you from taking a stand and changing strategies in response to your beloved fool's tactics. Take some time now to write down any new ideas God has impressed on you as you've read and studied. It's time for action!

New Strategy #1:

New Strategy #2:

New Strategy #3:

For the waywardness of the simple will kill them,
and the complacency of fools will destroy them;
but whoever listens to me will live in safety
and be at ease, without fear of harm.

PROVERBS 1:32-33

The only way of knowing a person
is to love them without hope.

WALTER BENJAMIN

There is a kind of release that comes directly to those
who have undergone an ordeal
and who know, having survived it,
that they are equal to all of life's occasions.

LEWIS MUMFORD

The best thing about the future is that it comes
one day at a time.

ABRAHAM LINCOLN

CHAPTER TEN

Letting Go When You Want to Hang On

If your fool has been a central concern in your life, not just the bane of your existence, then you have probably assumed a role that is extremely uncomfortable but that you have learned to play well: the role of savior.

Think about it. A savior, as we Christians define the role, is one who willingly gives of himself to save others who are wretched and blind and have no idea they need to be saved. They walk in darkness, and the savior brings light. They grovel in their sin while the savior hangs on a cross and dies for them. The savior cries, "Father forgive them for they know not what they do," and they laugh and try to make a profit on his clothes. He is wisdom in the face of foolishness, and because he loves, he allows himself to be destroyed so that they might have peace with God.

This is the role of the Savior. It has been played once on the stage of history, and there has been no curtain call. The part need never be played again. Yet what have you done for your fool by trying to "save" him from his own foolishness? Have you lost yourself trying somehow to make things right for this difficult person? Have you allowed your personhood to be sublimated by your fool's anger and hostility? Have you "given of yourself" with the thought that you can save your fool from his folly?

Have you suffered loss while your fool rages or laughs and walks away? Have you allowed yourself to be almost destroyed just to win peace with your fool? If so, you have assumed a position way out of your league.

There is a great passage in the book of Isaiah that beams a clear light on the foolishness of believing that you can save your fool or that you can survive his destructive behavior. Read it carefully, and let its truth soak into your heart.

> Thus says the LORD, the King of Israel
> And his Redeemer, the LORD of hosts:
> "I am the first and I am the last,
> *And there is no God besides Me.*
> And who is like Me? Let him proclaim and declare it;
> Yes, let him recount it to Me in order,
> From the time that I established the ancient nation.
> And let them declare to them the things that are coming
> And the events that are going to take place.
> Do not tremble and do not be afraid;
> Have I not long since announced it to you and declared it?
> And you are My witnesses.
> Is there any God besides Me,
> Or is there any other Rock?
> *I know of none."*
>
> (Isaiah 44:6-8, NASB, emphasis added)

If you are controlled by a fool, don't be afraid; there is a God who knows and understands. As you let go, you will find him more than capable of taking care of you and taking care of your fool. If you are hoping that by being a selfless martyr you are going to change your fool, then hope on, my friend. Martyrs don't change fools, only God does.

CHANGE BOTH OF YOU BY LETTING GO

If you have taken on the roles of critic, judge, savior, and protector in your attempts to control your fool, then you have probably become pretty crazy and out of control yourself. When you realize that your life, your thoughts, your prayers, and your personality are dominated by your fool, you'll probably say to yourself, *I have to change!* But you cannot change unless you alter the way you relate to your fool. It is imperative that you let go. When you let go, you are admitting there is nothing *you* can do to change your difficult person.

You may be thinking, *Let go? If I let go, everything will fall apart. I can't let go. What will happen if I do?* That's a great question. But it's one you can't answer, and neither can anyone else. The only thing you can know is that if you let go, you are making a positive step toward freeing yourself from the complications and chaos that bind you, and you're releasing your fool to the natural consequences of his foolish behavior. When you see the source of your problems and are willing to admit that only God can change your fool, you will have stepped out of denial into reality, where only God can work. By letting go, you remove yourself from the fool's realm of influence and you give up responsibility for your fool. It is a conscious effort on your part as well as an act of faith.

If you let go of the fool at your workplace and trust God, he will either change you or move you. He is too good and too faithful to leave you stuck in the mess one minute longer than necessary. He has assured us, "For I know the plans that I have for you,...plans for welfare and not for calamity to give you a future and a hope" (Jeremiah 29:11, NASB).

If you let go of your foolish parent and trust God to take care of him while he faithfully parents you, you will be amazed at how it changes you. Along with the psalmist you will be able to say, "For my father and my mother have forsaken me, but the LORD will take me up" (Psalm 27:10, NASB).

If you let go of your foolish mate and release him to his own devices, God will either give you the grace to endure or the grounds to be released from your vows.

If you let go of your foolish child and leave him to God, who judges righteously, you can be sure God will handle that child with equal amounts of love and justice. You can't know what God will do, but you can be assured that he will remain faithful to his Word, which tells us, "The Lord is not slow about His promise, as some count slowness, but is patient toward you, not wishing for any to perish but for all to come to repentance" (2 Peter 3:9, NASB)

If you let go of your foolish siblings you have felt responsible for all your life, God will meet those sisters or brothers where they are. With you out of the way, they will have to face the fact that not only are you no longer there to be responsible for them but that they must face God and his holiness on their own. As they do, they can be encouraged to know that "since He Himself was tempted in that which He has suffered, He is able to come to the aid of those who are tempted" (Hebrews 2:18, NASB).

Please notice that in none of these situations are you the change-agent or the need-meeter for your fool. When you release your fool, you embark on a journey of faith. You say in your heart, *I am going to trust God and look to him alone to be my source and resource. I will keep my focus on him!* That clear decision will leave your fool alone with God. When you stop playing the role of your fool's savior, doormat, and guardian angel all rolled into one, you will see that the stark reality of being left alone to face God will have an impact on him, if anything is going to.

As hard as it may be to face, the most hopeful reality your fool can experience is the realization that *Nobody cares about me but God.* Amidst all of his foolish thinking and destructive behavior, the fool has been able to deny that he has a problem, partially because you and others have gone along with him, believing you can change, influence, assist, or even force him to be a different person. If you will determine to remove your fool from the center of your attention by detaching and leaving him in God's hands, then and only then will you see what God can do.

KINGS AND PRODIGALS

Daniel 4:27-35 gives us a dramatic picture of a self-trusting fool who encountered the living God and was truly changed. King Nebuchadnezzar was surely one of the biggest fools who ever lived. It had been made clear to him that God had put him in his place of power, but the king's memory was short and his pride was tall. He became quite enamored with himself.

One day he was looking over Babylon and began to crow like a rooster! "This is the Babylon that I have made," he boasted. But before his last word left his lips, he knew it was the wrong thing to say. A voice from heaven boomed, in so many words, "That's it! Your power is no longer in effect. I'm sending you off for a long time until you can get this whole thing back into perspective."

And indeed, it *was* a long time. For seven years, King Neb was removed from his people, ate grass like an animal, and was totally bereft of the personal pampering to which he'd become accustomed. His hair grew long until it looked like eagles' feathers, and his fingernails became like claws. He was unrecognizable as the "great" man he had once been.

But according to his own account, King Neb came to his senses.

"I've got it now! God is right, and I am wrong! He's in charge of the whole world, and I'm not. He does what he wants to do, and I do what he wants me to do!" The king emerged from his time of madness with a whole new perspective on life. No longer was he the man he used to be. Finally he understood that there was a God—and he wasn't it!

You may be thinking, *Well, my fool isn't as bad as King Neb, and I surely don't want my fool to eat grass like a cow and have the dew turn his hair into eagles' feathers.* I understand, but what *would* you be willing for your fool to endure in order to leave behind his foolishness? What would you be willing to release to God in order for your fool to be changed?

Luke 15:11-32 tells the story of a father who had a foolish son. The father was faced with either letting his beloved son go or trying to keep him at home where he could protect him a little while longer and see if the lad might become wiser in time. When the boy, forever known as the Prodigal Son, got a burr under his saddle to go "be a man," he asked his father to cough up his inheritance early. He was tired of having to live as a son in his father's house. He wanted to go see what the world was really like. Things at home were too boring.

No sooner did the money hit his pocket than he packed up and headed for a far country. When he got there, he had a blast. He met some real sophisticates who knew how to experience life. They were his friends—until the money ran out. At the same time this happened, a great famine hit the land. (With God, timing is everything!) The boy who had never wanted for anything suddenly found himself hungry— so hungry that he was willing to eat the pods fed to the pigs he was hired to look after. Under those circumstances it didn't take long for this worldly wise, high-living man to wake up and come to his senses. He said to himself, "My father's hired men have more than enough to eat, and here I am eating pig slop!"

So, not being one to stay where things were tough, he got up and went home. But he was a totally changed young man. He had become a man willing to admit he had sinned against God and his father. He knew he was no longer worthy to be called his father's son. He knew he didn't deserve anything, and he wasn't looking for a handout anymore. He just wanted to come home.

But the father who loved him enough to let him go "saw him, and felt compassion for him, and ran and embraced him, and kissed him" (verse 20, NASB). The father interrupted his son's heartfelt apology with passionate words of joy and celebration. He called to his servants, "Quickly bring out the best robe and put it on him, and put a ring on his hand and sandals on his feet; and bring the fattened calf, kill it, and let us eat and be merry; for this son of mine was dead, and has come to life again; he was lost, and has been found" (verses 22-24, NASB). And then they partied!

THE ULTIMATE SURRENDER

Many prodigals are fools. They believe they are their own source and resource, and therefore they don't have to do things like other people. That's why the very best thing you can do for them is to let them go and allow natural consequences to wise them up.

Ruth Bell Graham wrote a wonderful book entitled *Prodigals and Those Who Love Them* (Focus on the Family Publishing, 1991). In it she said, "We cannot convict of sin, create hunger and thirst after God, or convert. These are miracles, and miracles are not in our department." She then listed the things we *can* do (the possible) and those things we must leave to God (the impossible). Applying those same categories to our fools helps us realize we can love, pray, and provide for legitimate needs, but we cannot enlighten or save them. That is God's job. The only hope for your fool—and for you—lies in surrendering him into the hands of God. He is fully capable of doing everything that needs to be done to turn your fool around. "The king's heart is like channels of water in the hand of the LORD; He turns it wherever He wishes" (Proverbs 21:1, NASB).

If releasing your fool into God's care is the ultimate surrender, then why does it sometimes feel that letting him go is wrong? That feeling may come as your fool protests the change of attitude he senses in you. Your fool may accuse you of abandoning him, complain that you are changing in ways he doesn't like, verbally or emotionally assault you for your failure to live up to his expectations, or pull away from you with a punishing silence. To be sure, the fool in your life will not look kindly on your change, because for you to change means that he is no longer in control. Consequently, he will respond with anger in one form or another.

It is important to recognize what your fool's anger is all about and why it has no power to harm you. Your fool wants to control, so when you leave him to face God and the consequences alone, the fool's anger will have lost some of its punch. He will become uncomfortable. This may intensify your difficulty for a while, but if you are committed to being a wise person, you will remain steadfast. When you are rejected, badgered, raged at, or manipulated, you will be able to persevere in the course you have chosen if you remember there is great purpose in what you are doing. You are seeking wisdom and a life that pleases God, *and* you are providing a clear shot for God to deal directly with your fool. When you choose to turn from being consumed by the behavior of your fool and begin to seek wisdom in everything you do, you will find new power—a strength that only God can give as you seek him rather than grope to settle things for yourself.

It's easy to become so consumed with your fool that you forget there is another realm where a heavenly Father who is intimately interested in the well-being of both you and your fool presides over everything that concerns you. He promises that he will cause all of this to work together for good. Not that your situation is good—it never is when you are entangled with a fool. But God promises to get involved and cause good for you if you are one of his. That is his legacy for his children.

And that, my friend, is why turning away from your fool in order to refocus on God and yourself is so important. Have you spent so much time enmeshed with your fool and his crazy-making behavior that you have neglected the most important things in life? Have you worked so hard to make peace with your fool that you have missed making peace with God? If living with your fool is the most important thing in your life, then that is what your life will contain. If living with God is the most important thing in your life, then quite quickly your perspective on your fool changes.

You have a great need, and there is only one who can meet that need! Only God can take care of you, and only God can be the savior in your fool's life. If you continue to assume any other stance than that, you will remain off balance and live at the mercy of your fool.

I encourage you to remember the words of Daniel: "But the people who know their God will display strength and take action" (11:32, NASB). If you know your God, then you can safely let go of your fool, replacing futile, frustrating effort with strength and action that is in the best interest of both yourself and the fool you love.

Vicky is a recovering fool whose mother did all she could do to raise her to be a young woman who loved God and was a credit to her family. Unfortunately, however, Vicky made some very naive and eventually habitual foolish choices that left her unable to think and reason maturely. Eventually she found herself in jail serving a year-long sentence.

The story of how Vicky became a fool and what finally pulled her from the pit is a classic. When she was a teenager, her dad left the family to pursue his own way with another woman. He continued to stay in close contact with Vicky, not for her sake but for his. He used her as a complaint department for all of his ills. Although she was hurt and angry with both her parents, Vicky felt the need to fix her dad. Her mother and other people who cared about her tried to reason with her, but she stubbornly believed that she knew the answers, particularly when it came to taking care of her dad's problems.

Vicky's anger toward everyone grew, and she began to lash out in rebellion, doing embarrassing things to make her mother look bad. She attached herself to the most obnoxious, twisted, angry people she could find and became at home in their group. After years of being pulled to pieces by her foolish dad, Vicky had succumbed to being a bona fide fool herself. She didn't want help, didn't need advice, and believed she could meet her own needs.

Only when she was caught in a car that was involved in a robbery did she find herself without answers. She couldn't talk her way out of the situation, although she tried to charm the bail bondsman and almost succeeded until a police officer stepped in. Once arrested, she was confined to an ugly world and surrounded by people who were as angry as she. Inside the jail, no one cared. The guards didn't express any concern or sympathy, and the other inmates were so caught up in their own complaints and defensiveness that they surely didn't want to be bothered with Vicky and her sad tale.

Vicky's mother visited once a week and brought inspirational books and Bible studies along with news from home. She didn't blame her daughter, pity her, or tell her she didn't belong there. She treated her kindly but made it clear that her own life was going on apart from her daughter's crisis. Vicky's life could be fulfilling too; it was all up to her. Vicky's mom had wised up; she was no longer trying to change her precious fool, nor was she allowing her fool to control her life.

Hemmed in by walls that wouldn't yield to her demands, surrounded by people who didn't care whether she lived or died, and loved by a mother who could no longer be manipulated, Vicky was left with only two ways to go. She could turn toward the God her mother had raised her to honor, or she could continue to do what she had been doing for so long: running her own life. For several months Vicky tried to blame everyone she knew for her anger and her predicament, but eventually, in the cold dampness of winter, Vicky cried out to God and admitted that she had become a fool. She looked around and realized she had come to live in a house of fools. She begged God to forgive her and to free her from the pit she had dug with her own hands.

Stuck between the pages of her childhood Bible her mom had brought to her in jail was a clipping from a Sunday school newspaper. Shortly after she cried out to God, Vicky found the little slip of paper on which Corrie ten Boom was quoted as saying: "There is no pit so deep that He is not deeper still!" Vicky also recalled a Scripture passage she had memorized as a little girl: "Trust in the LORD with all your heart and lean not on your own understanding; in all your ways acknowledge him, and he will make your paths straight (Proverbs 3:5-6). Suddenly the words learned long ago brimmed with comfort and seemed to offer Vicky a new kind of hope.

Today Vicky is slowly recovering her life and discovering the woman she was always intended to be before she took matters into her own hands. She has reconciled with her mother, and they talk regularly. The infrequent contacts with her father are detached. She has come to realize that she is unable to make his life better or fix him where he is broken. Vicky was a fool who is in the process of becoming wise.

Foolproofing your life is a serious pursuit but not a hopeless one. It is an individual journey to be taken one step at a time. When you become responsible for *yourself*, submit yourself to the God who made you, and release your beloved fool into the Savior's hands, you will be amazed at what he will do both with your fool and with you.

In the book of Jeremiah God speaks about his people and his plans for them. If you are one of his people, he says, "'You will seek me and find me when you seek me with all your heart. I will be found by you,' declares the LORD, 'and will bring you back from captivity'" (Jeremiah 29:13-14).

Our God is a God of miracles who can and will do what is good. He asks you to trust him even when it doesn't look like he's moving an inch! I pray that you will be able to become a person of freedom and honesty as you move along your path toward wholeness. I know and believe that as you fully submit to the awesome power of God, you can be free of the controlling power of your fool because "'God opposes the proud but gives grace to the humble.' Humble yourselves, therefore, under God's mighty hand, that he may lift you up in due time. Cast all your anxiety on him because he cares for you" (1 Peter 5:5-7).

The journey has been long as you have approached the "jumping-off point." This is the test of all that you believe. Letting go is the hardest challenge you face because it requires you to lay down every weapon, hook, rope, cord, or device you have for maintaining control! When you let go, you determine to trust that God himself will faithfully handle whatever situation your letting go creates.

No longer are your eyes riveted on your fool. No longer are your ears attuned to what your fool might say or might intend by what he says. No longer are you defined by what your fool says you are. No longer do you freely believe whatever your fool says about you or about himself. You have arrived at a new place, and here the only focus you can have if you want to maintain your newfound sanity is your focus on God. It is time to silence the voices of people who are telling you that you're doing it all wrong. It is time to put your faith in God alone.

Think About It

Read Psalm 25:1-9 and make it the prayer of your life as we explore the ultimate challenge of "letting go." Note in the margin the specific requests that are made.

To you, O LORD, I lift up my soul;
  in you I trust, O my God.
Do not let me be put to shame,
  nor let my enemies triumph over me.
No one whose hope is in you

will ever be put to shame,
but they will be put to shame
who are treacherous without excuse.
Show me your ways, O LORD,
teach me your paths;
guide me in your truth and teach me,
for you are God my Savior,
and my hope is in you all day long.
Remember, O LORD, your great mercy and love,
for they are from of old.
Remember not the sins of my youth
and my rebellious ways;
according to your love remember me,
for you are good, O LORD.
Good and upright is the LORD;
therefore he instructs sinners in his ways.
He guides the humble in what is right
and teaches them his way.

1. List the questions you have for the Lord regarding the process of surrender.

2. What is the hardest part of letting go for you? Why?

3. Where do you expect to be in your life and in your relationships a year from now? (Put a date beside the answer so you can refer back to it in a year.)

Go to God About It

Spend some time meditating on the following verses, trying to settle once and for all what it means to entrust to the Lord your fool and all that he represents.

Isaiah 44:8
Do not tremble, do not be afraid.
  Did I not proclaim this and foretell it long ago?
You are my witnesses. Is there any God besides me?
  No, there is no other Rock; I know not one.

Psalm 62:5-7
Find rest, O my soul, in God alone;
  my hope comes from him.
He alone is my rock and my salvation;
  he is my fortress, I will not be shaken.
My salvation and my honor depend on God;
  he is my mighty rock, my refuge.

The antics of your fool no longer need to seem so overpowering. No longer will his definition of you apply. No longer will your emotions be fair game for your fool's combat boots to stomp. You are a different person now because you are accessing the power and the protection of the God who indwells you!

Consult the Bible About It

If you're afraid that your problem is too big, too complex, or too long-standing for God to handle, take a deep breath and see what Scripture tells us about him.

Isaiah 40:25-31

"To whom will you compare me?
     Or who is my equal?" says the Holy One.
Lift your eyes and look to the heavens:
     Who created all these?
He who brings out the starry host one by one,
     and calls them each by name.
Because of his great power and mighty strength,
     not one of them is missing.
Why do you say, O Jacob,
     and complain, O Israel,
"My way is hidden from the LORD;
     my cause is disregarded by my God"?
Do you not know?
     Have you not heard?
The LORD is the everlasting God,
     the Creator of the ends of the earth.

He will not grow tired or weary,
>   and his understanding no one can fathom.
He gives strength to the weary
>   and increases the power of the weak.
Even youths grow tired and weary,
>   and young men stumble and fall;
but those who hope in the LORD
>   will renew their strength.
They will soar on wings like eagles;
>   they will run and not grow weary,
>   they will walk and not be faint.

1. List the things you just learned about the Holy One.

2. What does he tell you to do?

3. When you let go, to whom are you handing over the reins?

4. Does God need your help? Why or why not?

What Will You Do About It?

Why not turn to the prayer you pasted in the front of this book and see what you wrote as you were starting this journey? What do you think as you look at your own words?

Take a few moments to add whatever you might want to at this point on the path toward wisdom. Date your addition, and as you close this book on foolproofing your life, thank God that you are no longer a hostage of a fool. You are free! And now God finally has an opportunity to do what only he can do in the life of your beloved fool. He or she is God's problem now—totally and completely God's. You have only one job: to focus on your Lord and ask him each day, "What do you want me to do today, Lord? I am yours."

QUESTIONS & ANSWERS
Ten Tough Dilemmas About Life with a Fool

When I speak or counsel on the topic of foolproofing your life, several tough questions arise over and over again. Because no one book can (or should) tell you exactly what to do about complex relational issues, you are probably left with some questions and dilemmas as you finish this book. How can you relate more wisely to *your* fool and his or her particular characteristics? What is the best course to take as you continue your journey toward change?

Below I've attempted to answer the most common questions I'm asked when I present what I've learned about fools and foolproofing. I realize the limitation of answering questions in a format that does not allow interaction, and I'm sure there will be "but what if?" questions that come to your mind. That's when you'll have the privilege and comfort of turning to the Wonderful Counselor who will give you divine guidance if you prayerfully seek his will.

I hope that you are wiser for this journey we have taken together and that along the way you have come to know yourself and your God far more intimately. My prayer for you comes from the book of Jude:

> But you, dear friends, build yourselves up in your most holy faith and pray in the Holy Spirit. Keep yourselves in God's love as you wait for the mercy of our Lord Jesus Christ to bring you to eternal life. Be merciful to those who doubt; snatch others from the fire and save them; to others show mercy, mixed with fear—hating even the clothing stained by corrupted flesh. To

him who is able to keep you from falling and to present you before his glorious presence without fault and with great joy—to the only God our Savior be glory, majesty, power and authority, through Jesus Christ our Lord, before all ages, now and forevermore! Amen. (verses 20-25)

1. Can a fool be a Christian?

The person who asks this question usually wants to believe that his or her fool is simply a deceived believer who has "backslidden" or who just never grew to maturity. Well, I have looked and looked for that kind of believer in Scripture, because if that were true, so many questions and problems might be cleared up. I am convinced by my study of the Word, however, that even if this person is the biggest churchgoer in town, if he repeatedly displays the classic foolish thinking and behavior patterns described in this book, then the person can't be a believer who is "born again."

Consider Galatians 5:19-24:

Now the deeds of the flesh are evident, which are: immorality, impurity, sensuality, idolatry, sorcery, enmities, strife, jealousy, outbursts of anger, disputes, dissensions, factions, envying, drunkenness, carousing, and things like these, of which I forewarn you just as I have forewarned you that those who practice such things shall not inherit the kingdom of God. But the fruit of the Spirit is love, joy, peace, patience, kindness, goodness, faithfulness, gentleness, self-control; against such things there is no law. Now those who belong to Christ Jesus have crucified the flesh with its passions and desires. (NASB)

Note the marks of protracted, habitual anger described in Galatians 5:19 (enmities, strife, jealousy, outbursts of anger, disputes, dissensions, factions), and then think back to all that Proverbs says about anger and the fool. Because anger is the fool's weapon of choice, you will find that is characteristic of how he behaves. These characteristics are described as the "deeds of the flesh," and if they occur habitually with no confession and no repentance, then clearly they come from someone who does not belong to God. Therefore, I would ask you, can a fool be a Christian?

Romans 1 describes the fools who "take it to the limit." Because they suppress the truth that God has plainly revealed to them and because "although they knew God, they neither glorified him as God nor gave thanks to him," their thinking became very muddled and "their foolish hearts were darkened" (verse 21). And in one bold statement, the Word proclaims, "Although they claimed to be wise, they became fools" (verse 22). Because of this, God gave them over to just do what they chose to do!

The strategic "indifference" of God is a terrible thing, but it is exactly what fools experience when they continue to insist on being in charge of their lives. And because God lets them do what they want without interference, they become eaten up with "envy, murder, strife, deceit and malice. They are gossips, slanderers, God-haters, insolent, arrogant and boastful; they invent ways of doing evil; they disobey their parents; they are senseless, faithless, heartless, ruthless. Although they know God's righteous decree that those who do such things deserve death, they not only continue to do these very things but also approve of those who practice them" (verse 29).

These are the kinds of people who say, "I'm going to split hell wide open, but at least I'll have lots of buddies!" They believe they shouldn't be questioned because they are always right. It's their way or no way. These people have said in their hearts, *There is no God.* This is the ultimate end for fools, unless at some point they recognize their folly and see that they have no choice but to repent, to have a change of mind with a change of direction.

Please note that I do not believe the fool is beyond redemption. Certainly not! But in order for a fool to be saved, God himself must reach down into the deepest pit, where every fool ends up, in order to offer a way of escape. You can't offer it, and neither can anyone else. You can pray for your fool, you can offer him the gospel, and you can live rightly before him. You will find, however, that in most situations all your efforts have little effect. The change in a fool's heart is one of those single-handed "God-moves" that requires supernatural intervention.

We do not know and we cannot tell when God's "giving someone over" to do what he wants to do turns into a permanent state where God has totally taken his hands off. That is a point only God can define. Until that time, there may be many dramatic, attention-grabbing events that will let the fool know the time for "wising up" is running out. Unfortunately, however, those events that would shake the nonfool to the very core often only harden the heart of the fool.

This "hardening" process is exemplified by Pharaoh in the Old Testament. He was holding the children of Israel captive and refused to let them go. God sent Moses to tell him what would happen if he didn't release God's people, but Pharaoh didn't believe Moses. Why should he? No one could tell him anything. Even when the plagues came and even when the Lord moved across the land taking the firstborn of every household, including Pharaoh's own, the foolish ruler still would not repent. Throughout the entire account, we are told that God "hardened Pharaoh's heart." The original language indicates that God strengthened the hardness that Pharaoh already had in his heart.

Pharaoh was a classic fool. His story shows us that when a fool stubbornly goes his own way, habitually refuses to bend his knee to God, and holds to his belief that he is his own source and resource, then at any point God may "give him over" to the path he has foolishly chosen. The fool has so hardened his own heart that he is only good for God to use as a pawn on a divine chessboard. At this point the fool has abdicated the possibility of salvation.

Read the account in Exodus 13 of what foolish Pharaoh did once he had let the people go out of Egypt. As you read the repeated statements that God hardened Pharaoh's heart, remember that his heart was already hardened; God just used the hardness for his glory. The word used for "harden" simply means "to make stronger." Pharaoh was already bent on mistreating the Israelites; God just "strengthened" his bent. I think it is clear that a person with a heart bent against God cannot be a Christian, no matter how righteous some of his external behaviors may appear.

2. How can I honor my father and mother when they qualify as fools?

What does it mean to "honor" one's parents? Perhaps they have behaved foolishly all of your life, but you have finally found healthy ways to relate to them by detaching, forgiving, and praying for them. Then you are told by a well-meaning friend or relative: "But you are supposed to 'honor' your father and mother." Inevitably this is said with a scowl of disapproval that leaves you confused and guilt-ridden. Just what *are* you supposed to do with your foolish parents? What does God expect?

First of all, you are to treat them differently than anyone else because God has assigned you the role of their son or daughter. It is your job to honor them, even if they are difficult and qualify as fools. In the Old Testament, the word *honor* means to give weight or value to. In other words, you are to treat them as valuable simply because they are your parents. If they need your help as they grow older, it is your responsibility to care for their physical needs. Although they may have proven that they are incapable or unwilling to parent *you*, you still are required to care for *them*. Just because they abdicated their parenting role long ago, you are not allowed to follow suit.

In the New Testament, Jesus spoke to the fools in his life, the Pharisees, who always trusted in their own hearts. When they asked him questions just to goad him, he responded to them this way:

> And why do you break the command of God for the sake of your tradition? For God said, "Honor your father and mother" and "Anyone who curses his father or mother must be put to death." But you say that if a man says to his father or mother, "Whatever help you might otherwise have received from me is a gift devoted to God," he is not to "honor his father" with it. (Matthew 15:3-6)

From these words you can deduce that you are not to speak evil of your parents and you are not to give away the resources you would ordinarily be able to use to help meet their legitimate needs. It is your role as a child to be responsible toward your parents, to not curse your mother or father, and to provide for their needs. Of course, even in this you must use wisdom. Scripture does not require you to be held hostage by anyone's foolish behavior. If, however, your parents have a legitimate need that they can't meet themselves, it is your obligation to meet it. Being emotionally intimate, spending a lot of time together, and being "one big happy family" is not required if it is not authentic; but being kind and meeting needs are. As long as you can detach, forgive, and pray, you should be able to find the balance that God requires as you obey his command to honor your parents, no matter how foolish they may be.

3. What if my fool is my adult child who is the parent of my grandchildren?

If you're dealing with an adult child who is a fool while you're trying to be a godly grandparent to your grandchildren, then I know you are in a very difficult situation. Proverbs 17 recognizes your situation with these words: "To have a fool for a son brings grief; there is no joy for the father of a fool…. A foolish son brings grief to his father and bitterness to the one who bore him" (verses 21,25).

There are several issues to consider, but one of the guiding principles you need to remember is that you cannot "fix" the situation. Once your children become adults, you no longer have the responsibility to play the role of parent. You are now responsible to relinquish that position for better or for worse and to allow your adult child to become responsible for himself or herself.

When your child fails to act responsibly, I know it's easy to lapse into the "fix-it" mode. And that's how your adult children learn to rely on you to take care of their needs, to be there for them, no matter what. The very things they need to be learning to take responsibility for and trust God for, they learn instead to demand from you. If your adult child is a fool, then we know he isn't going to rely on God and will only be happy with you as long as you're giving what he wants. As a result, it's easy for you to get into the habit of "performing" in order to keep everything peaceful.

Once grandchildren are added to the mix, you have a royal mess. You see the innocence of your grandchildren, and you don't want them to suffer because of the foolish choices of your child. So once again, you come to the rescue, and your fool is freed from his or her responsibilities.

So, what to do?

The wise path requires that you determine not to play God or be the "need-meeter" for your foolish child. You will make sure that your grandchildren know that they have a grandparent who prays for them and loves them dearly. But beyond that, if your foolish child is going to recognize and embrace responsibility for his children, then he must do it without your intervention. If failure results and you step in to assume your adult child's basic responsibilities as a parent, then it may become a matter for the law to deal with. No one wants to see the courts involved with his family, but if your child is so foolish as to abdicate responsibilities in a way that puts the children at risk, then it is best to have that behavior exposed and dealt with rather than for you to act as the rescuer.

I realize this is a simplistic answer for a very complex situation, but when you face the core facts about your fool's behavior, you aren't left with a host of options. You can choose to be the caretaker for your adult child and his children and be without recourse when the situation becomes unbearable. Or you can take the wiser path and draw some specific, strong boundaries, giving appropriate love and support to your grandchildren while loving your foolish child enough to allow God to deal with him as only God can. You can participate in the process by obeying the truth you know about being a righteous person. Proverbs 4:18-22 sums it up like this:

> The path of the righteous is like the first gleam of dawn,
>> shining ever brighter till the full light of day.
> But the way of the wicked is like deep darkness;
>> they do not know what makes them stumble.
> My son, pay attention to what I say;
>> listen closely to my words.
> Do not let them out of your sight,
>> keep them within your heart;

for they are life to those who find them

and health to a man's whole body.

You are to be the light in the situation, but you will be hard-pressed to shine if you keep the truth under wraps and take care of your fool by trying to fix everything.

4. What if I see my teenager becoming a fool?

It is agonizing to see a beloved child headed toward the sure destruction that awaits a fool. Although you talk, plead, correct, and pray, often there are no results. All you receive in return is the cold, steely stare of determined rebellion. You move from one crisis to another, hoping against hope that you will see dawn break the darkness. These are the times when you have to apply two truths that are universal in dealing with a fool. One is to pray for your teenager, and the second is to detach.

Immediately the question comes, "But how can I detach from my child?" Remember, detaching doesn't mean not caring; it is a wise strategy to preserve your sanity and to relinquish your beloved fool to God's care. If your teenager is demonstrating foolish tendencies, then he is probably expressing foolish anger toward you and disrespecting who you are. Teenagers believe they are right and they trust in their own counsel, so they disrespect the advice of their parents. When that kind of foolish thinking and behaving becomes habitual, chaos at home is the result.

Let me give you a case study that might shed some light on what you could do if you have a teenager headed up Fool's Mountain. Jeremy is the oldest of five children. His father divorced his mother in a fit of midlife insanity and personal foolishness. Jeremy was a witness to all that transpired, and he was deeply hurt by the whole thing. Although Jeremy's mother wanted the marriage to work, his dad was ready to move on to greener pastures.

Torn between the two parents he loved, Jeremy chose to live with his dad. The new freedom, the new things, and the new lifestyle were appealing to him and set him apart from his brothers and sisters. As time passed, Jeremy spent less and less time with his mother and siblings. It was difficult for his mother to see her sixteen-year-old child following in his father's footsteps. As her husband had been disrespectful and abusive to her, so her son became. Jeremy's brothers and sisters watched in dismay as Jeremy refused to do things with them when he came to the house, refused to eat with the family, hogged the TV remote control, and disrespectfully told his mother what he would and would not do.

Jeremy's mother loved him, and she loved God. She could not bear to watch her firstborn become a statistical tragedy. She was losing him, and she knew it. She determined that she would pray and seek the wisdom of God for her boy. One morning during her prayer time it came to her: *You have taken away every privilege in your attempts to discipline and shape your son. But he still has you. He has not lost everything.* That weekend, when Jeremy was on his usual tear around the house, his mother called him aside. "Jeremy," she explained, "I have taken away every privilege I can take from you. I have grounded you and told you 'no' more often than I have been able to say 'yes.' I love you, son, and I only have one thing left to take away from you, and that is me."

Stunned but still very cool, Jeremy shrugged. His mother continued talking, "So, from now on, you won't be allowed to come to the house unless you can speak respectfully to me and treat your brothers and sisters fairly."

Jeremy flipped off a rebellious "Cool," and said, "I'm going to Dad's." When he left, his mother's heart was breaking, but she knew if she would ever have her son back as a wise child, it would require extreme, very costly measures.

Several months passed, months filled with many lonely days of trusting God to work in her son's heart. Jeremy's mom wrote him notes about the family and assured him of her love on a regular basis, but she never asked him to come home. The only way back was with a changed attitude.

You may be saying, "But my fool lives at my house. I can't send him away." That's true, but consistent discipline is the only tool you have to use on a child who is looking for ways to act out his foolishness. Reasoning won't work, and typical behavior modification won't work, so you apply the discipline that cuts the deepest and then wait for God to do the difficult internal work that you cannot bring about. Allowing consequences to reign in full force is the most powerful decision you can make. If there is a scrape at school, a speeding ticket, recurring tardiness at work, or an infraction of the rules at home, let the full force of the situation pound your foolish child. While the consequences discipline him, your job is to beseech the Lord to use those circumstances to change your child.

Letting a fool "just be" while he is still under your roof and rule will more than likely end in grief. The Scriptures say, "Discipline your son, for in that there is hope; do not be a willing party to his death" (Proverbs 19:18). Another verse adds, " He who fears the LORD has a secure fortress, and for his children it will be a refuge" (Proverbs 14:26). For the teenager who can go either way, toward foolishness or toward wisdom, the strictest discipline is what you want to use. This is not a time for softness or weakness on your part. If you and your mate have a disagreement regarding appropriate discipline, I believe wisdom opts for the one parent who would go toward the "harder line." I don't mean harsh or abusive discipline but discipline that is just plain unbendable in the face of foolish rebellion. When you couple strong, consistent discipline with your own healthy fear of the Lord, you are offering your foolish child a chance to turn toward wisdom before he does major damage to himself and to the family.

Jeremy has "come to his senses" since the day his mother took a hard line with him. Wiser now, he has inched his way back home and often asks to visit his mother's house. He speaks respectfully to her and has stopped harassing his brothers and sisters. He still wants his independence (which is normal for an adolescent), but now he has seen that if he wants a relationship with his mother, it will be on terms that require him to lay aside his foolishness.

5. What is my role in regard to sexual intimacy when my spouse is my fool?
I am convinced that if you choose to remain with your mate, no matter how foolish he or she is, then sexual intimacy is part of the package. If you choose to separate from your mate with the goal of remaining unmarried or seeking reconciliation, then you are not responsible to fulfill the role of a wife or a husband by giving your body to your mate. Paul's teaching in 1 Corinthians 7:3-5 is clear:

> The husband should fulfill his marital duty to his wife, and likewise the wife to her husband. The wife's body does not belong to her alone but also to her husband. In the same way, the husband's body does not belong to him alone but also to his wife. Do not deprive each other except by mutual consent and for a time, so that you may devote yourselves to prayer. Then come together again so that Satan will not tempt you because of your lack of self-control.

I have had women tell me they feel like prostitutes when they have sex with their foolish husbands. I tell them I'm truly sorry they feel that way, but they must believe the truth: They are not prostitutes. Rather, they are fulfilling God's command, and as long as they are living within a marriage relationship, sexual intimacy is part of their role and responsibility.

You might take stock and ask yourself, *Am I doing everything I can to be at peace with my fool?* Sometimes we sabotage a tolerable coexistence by making demands or refusing to participate in the relationship because we are angry. In our heart of hearts we really want to punish our fools, but God calls us to be responsible for changing our part in the situation.

6. What do I do if my fool is an alcoholic or addict?

Active alcoholics and drug addicts usually display an array of foolish behaviors, but not all of these individuals are fools. Alcoholics or addicts who are open to help and are actively engaged in finding a way to deal with their alcoholism or addiction are not fools. However, if your alcoholic or addict rejects counsel, believes he can break the addiction alone, and expects you to go along with him, then you may have an alcoholic fool on your hands. The same principles of detachment, forgiveness, and prayer apply in this difficult situation.

Recognize as well that if your fool is an alcoholic or addict, then there are several components at work. The physical addiction is real. Your fool is physically sick, but you can't heal him. You also can't change the alcoholic's drinking behavior by being different yourself—no matter how much he may try to convince you that if you would just… That is part of the addict's con. Blame is not easy to deal with unless you know the truth, and the truth is that you are not responsible for your fool's alcoholism or addiction. If you want to remain free of the chaos that an alcoholic or addict's disease inflicts on everyone around him, then you must be aware that you cannot fix the problem, and the more uninvolved you can be the better.

If your addicted fool is your mate, the principle to apply is to live at peace or to live alone with a heart for reconciliation and a will to remain single. If your alcoholic fool is your parent, the principle is to not speak ill of him but to provide what you can if the parent has a need he cannot meet independently. (Be careful of being conned!) If your addicted fool is your child, the principle is to love and pray but allow the consequences of the child's choices to drive him to the end of himself. Loving and praying in this way is actually the most dynamic thing you can do. If your alcoholic fool is a more distant family member, treat the relative like a stranger. Be detached, be polite, and release him to face the consequences. God is free to do his very best work when we get out of the way! If your addicted fool is a friend or coworker, keep your distance and avoid becoming entangled. As with the relative, be polite, be detached, and don't be conned into being part of the problem by enabling him to fall deeper into his addiction and all the foolishness that comes with it.

7. *What about all the directives in Scripture about turning the other cheek and loving my neighbor? As a Christian, am I not supposed to love my fool unconditionally and forgive him "seventy times seven"?*
Loving unconditionally doesn't mean loving without a brain! Remember, Scripture says, "He who walks with the wise grows wise, but a companion of fools suffers harm" (Proverbs 13:20). If love really is unconditional, then it does what is in the ultimate best interest of the other person. Often what we call "love" is just an emotion we have and an action we do to keep peace with a quarrelsome person. But if real love

seeks another's highest good, then to love a fool is to do whatever has to be done so he can see the foolishness and abandon it. Only then might the fool turn toward God to meet his needs. Leaving the fool alone to face the consequences of his own foolish choices often is required. As long as you are busy trying to keep peace where there is no peace, your fool misses out on facing the consequences and turning to God.

You can fulfill the biblical command to "turn the other cheek" by refusing to strike back at your fool, to quarrel, to engage in strife. That doesn't mean you go to your fool and say, "Hit me!" That is foolish. If, however, your fool does strike you emotionally or physically, it means that you refuse to become like him. Refuse to strike back, and stand a little farther away the next time you meet! Remember the drawbridge that gives entrance to your castle? Use it wisely.

As for forgiveness, of course you forgive (relinquish your right to punish), but you don't expect or even try to have a satisfying, intimate relationship. With a fool who is his own source and resource, such a relationship is impossible. When you forgive your fool, you demonstrate your own relationship with God and make room for God to change your fool.

A fool will probably not notice or appreciate your forgiveness or godly character, but God notices. You are to behave in a truly Christian way toward your fool, including taking a hard line for his good because you *are* a Christian and your responsibility is to honor God by loving as he loves. Your fool's response is not the issue; your own integrity and obedience are.

8. If I go for counseling, what kind of counselor should I seek?

If you are going to emerge from the relationship with your fool as a whole person, you need to be careful about the counsel you receive.

Unless the one counseling you understands who you are dealing with and what makes him tick, you may not get good advice, even though the counselor may be godly and well-intentioned. It is critical that you find a wise counselor who knows Scripture and what it says about fools. Just because someone's shingle has an icthus or a cross on it, don't assume that he or she will counsel you from a biblical perspective.

Also be aware that religious counsel can sometimes be rigid counsel. Just because a counselor has the Bible, it doesn't mean he has the wisdom of God or the spirit of Jesus of whom it was said, "A bruised reed he will not break, and a smoldering wick he will not snuff out" (Isaiah 42:3). I shudder when I hear a religious person throwing the statement "God hates divorce" on the back of someone in a troubled marriage, or even worse, on the back of someone who has gone through a divorce. Having worked with so many in this situation, I can tell you, no one hates divorce more than the divorced! No one finds joy in the demise of a marriage, and a wise counselor does not use Scripture as a weapon.

If you are seeking counsel for coping with your fool, don't stop until you find someone who loves God *and* people. If a counselor's sole purpose is to impose his perception of "God's ways" on you without having the same compassion God has for you, then you will find yourself in an impossible situation. The person you want to find is one who has a healthy reverence for God and a deep understanding of his wisdom.

The following story is the sad commentary of a woman who failed to find a wise counselor. Barbara's husband, Ray, was openly sleeping with another woman. He told Barbara he was through with their marriage and wanted out. Barbara filed for divorce and then went to see a religious counselor at the request of a friend. Before she left the session that day, the counselor insisted that Barbara call her attorney and call off the divorce. Under great duress, Barbara did just that.

Unfortunately, nothing changed with her husband. Ray continued to sleep with his new love. The only effect of calling off the divorce was that it cost Barbara several hundred dollars. The initial retainer she paid the lawyer was lost, and when it was evident Ray had no intention of changing, she had to refile and spend several hundred more dollars. The religious counselor was not out any money and did not have to walk in Barbara's shoes through the whole sordid mess. All the counselor did was to use the Bible without thinking, without really seeking God's wisdom. She simply determined that because Malachi 2:16 says God hates divorce then God must not want Barbara to seek one. No consideration was given to this admonition, which God gave to all husbands, including Barbara's:

> Let your fountain be blessed,
> And rejoice in the wife of your youth.
> As a loving hind and a graceful doe,
> Let her breasts satisfy you at all times;
> Be exhilarated always with her love.
> For why should you, my son, be exhilarated with an adulteress,
> And embrace the bosom of a foreigner?
> For the ways of a man are before the eyes of the LORD,
> And He watches all his paths.
> His own iniquities will capture the wicked,
> And he will be held with the cords of his sin.
> He will die for lack of instruction,
> And in the greatness of his folly he will go astray.
>
> (Proverbs 5:18-23, NASB)

Unfortunately, Barbara's counselor didn't look deeper and consider the whole counsel of the Word, including the words of Jesus when he said, "Because of your hardness of heart, Moses permitted you to divorce your wives; but from the beginning it has not been this way. And I say to you, whoever divorces his wife, except for immorality, and marries another woman commits adultery" (Matthew 19:8-9, NASB).

Ray had divorce in his heart. He was sleeping with another woman and wanted to marry another woman. Because of the hardness of his heart, Barbara had permission from God to divorce. The covenant between them was broken. But Barbara was bludgeoned with the pseudowisdom of the religious counselor who took God's Word out of context. Read the following words from Malachi 2:16 in context, and consider what you would have said to Barbara.

> "For I hate divorce," says the LORD, the God of Israel, *"and him who covers his garment with wrong,"* says the LORD of hosts. "So take heed to your spirit, *that you do not deal treacherously."* (NASB, emphasis added)

It is interesting to note that no one ever considered the fact that Barbara was entangled with a fool. The counselor's only interest was to "salvage the marriage." The truth was, there was no marriage to be salvaged! Rather, there was a legal agreement that was regularly defied by the guilty party, and yet the counselor created a burden for the innocent party. Jesus offered a bearable burden when he said, "For my yoke is easy and my burden is light" (Matthew 11:30). The obligations God requires us to keep are not great burdens that weigh us down and break us.

Before you commit to spending a lot of time with a counselor, ask yourself, *Am I comfortable with this individual?* And ask him or her some specific questions. If you have determined that you might be entangled with a fool, be up-front and ask what your counselor knows about the teachings of the book of Proverbs. His answer could be the deciding point for you. If the counselor misses the fact that you are dealing with a bona fide fool as defined by God, then he may instruct you to apply conventional skills and to seek reconciliation before there is a major God-alteration in your fool and some honest God-probing in your own life. If the counselor does not have the full picture of what you're up against and is not equipped to offer you biblical counsel, find someone who is.

9. I feel so guilty for the foolish things I have done in my relationship to my fool. I can't forgive myself.

If you feel guilty, then you are not alone. Trying to relate to a fool, to keep him or her happy, and to create peace with someone who doesn't desire peace can cause you to do many things you later regret. If others were involved who suffered because you were trying to mollify your fool, then that creates guilt in your life too.

Choices are a serious matter, and when they have been made under the influence of a fool, the consequences can be terrible to contemplate. Cynthia's children bore the brunt of the foolish choices she made in response to the beloved fools in her life. Thinking she was doing the right thing by allowing her mother and father to live in her house (even though they were perfectly healthy) created a crazy situation for her family. Cynthia's father is a "happy alcoholic" who drinks every night from five o'clock on. He never abuses anyone, but he becomes very loud, talkative, and dominating. The whole family is influenced by his behavior. Cynthia's mother is a nervous sort who covers for her husband's slurred speech and annoying ways. Dinner at Cynthia's house is always a nerve-racking affair.

The children grew up in this environment where Cynthia defended her parents while they carried on their nightly charade. The children's father, Wes, simply sat in stony silence through the whole ordeal. When the children got old enough, they both left home immediately, declaring they had had enough. "You can live in this insanity if you want to, Mom, but I'm outta here." Those were the words of her beloved Rodney, whom she had always assumed to be rolling with the punches. She hadn't been as surprised when Cindy Rose left home and rarely called, but when Rodney gave his farewell statement, Cynthia was devastated.

When Cynthia allowed her parents to move in with her and her husband six years after they were married, she didn't count the cost. Now, twelve years later, she realizes what that move has done to her family, and there is no recalling the years. Oh, she feels sure that Rodney, and probably Cindy Rose, will come around when they get older, but she's not sure what will happen with Wes. His distance is palpable. He is physically faithful, but it seems that his heart has checked out. Every evening as the two couples have dinner together, Wes floats off into his own world, never participating in the conversation. Cynthia's dad says enough for everyone while her mother fidgets and tries to keep things at a low roar.

Cynthia has asked Wes's forgiveness and has contacted both of the children and asked their forgiveness as well. They say they forgive her, but she can't really believe them. She can't receive anyone's forgiveness because she can't forgive herself. She knows Wes and the kids will "recover" and go on with life, but she can't believe she was so foolish as to take her parents in when they didn't even need to live there. She just thought it would help her mother manage her father and that her husband and kids wouldn't mind. Actually, she hadn't really considered what they would feel. All during her childhood she had played the role of the "fix-it girl" in response to her dad's buffoonery and her mom's fragility, and it only seemed normal to continue doing so when she grew up. Now she knows she was wrong. She was weak when she should have been strong, and the people she loved the most in the world were adversely affected by her foolish choices. Now she can't forgive herself.

When I talked with Cynthia, she was shredding a tissue as she fidgeted through the whole story. When she finished, I asked, "What makes you think you can forgive yourself? Did you know that is one of the things God tells us we cannot do? Nowhere in Scripture does it say that we are to forgive ourselves."

Cynthia looked surprised as I explained, "God tells us that *he* has forgiven us. That was accomplished by Jesus' death on the cross. All the wrath God had stored up to be poured out on your sin and on mine was poured out on Jesus Christ as he hung dying. God's Word says that 'in him [Jesus Christ] we have redemption through his blood, the forgiveness of sins, in accordance with the riches of God's grace' [Ephesians 1:7]. That's what God has done for us—and he is the only one who can do it!"

Remember the story in Mark 2 about the paralytic man who was let down through the roof by his friends? When Jesus saw him and saw his friends' faith, he said to the paralytic, "Son, your sins are forgiven" (verse 5). Immediately after this declaration of grace, some of the religious folks present got hot under the collar, as the rest of the story reveals:

> Now some teachers of the law were sitting there, thinking to themselves, "Why does this fellow talk like that? He's blaspheming! Who can forgive sins but God alone?"

Immediately Jesus knew in his spirit that this was what they were thinking in their hearts, and he said to them, "Why are you thinking these things? Which is easier: to say to the paralytic, 'Your sins are forgiven,' or to say, 'Get up, take your mat and walk'? But that you may know that the Son of Man has authority on earth to forgive sins...." He said to the paralytic, "I tell you, get up, take your mat and go home." He got up, took his mat and walked out in full view of them all. This amazed everyone and they praised God, saying, "We have never seen anything like this!" (verses 6-12)

You see, that is the miracle of forgiveness extended to us through Christ. Only he can forgive sins. There just isn't any place where we are told, "And don't forget to forgive yourself too!" Our guilt can be removed only by accepting the gift of God's forgiveness. The only thing we can do to complete the process of forgiveness in our lives is to agree with God that we have sinned. The rest is up to him. First John 1:8-9 tells us, "If we claim to be without sin, we deceive ourselves and the truth is not in us. If we confess our sins, he is faithful and just and will forgive us our sins and purify us from all unrighteousness."

If you have been relating to a fool, living in a foolish situation, and responding foolishly, then you can't escape feeling guilty. Yet there is nothing you can do to "clean up the past" except agree with God that you have sinned and then accept the fact that you are forgiven. You may not feel forgiven. You may not even see yourself as forgiven. But God says you are forgiven, so you can abandon the quest of trying to forgive yourself. Once you abandon yourself utterly to God's grace, he will remove your sin and sweep away your guilt.

10. Suppose my fool surprises me and says he is wrong and wants to work things out. What should I do?

When someone truly repents (agrees that he is wrong and then wants to go in another direction), you will see an attitude of humility. An individual who has maintained his position for an extended period of time, has been his own "god," and has sought no one else's counsel will definitely demonstrate an attitude change if he is sincere about repenting. His attitude will be like that of a servant. Realizing that he has been wrong and has hurt you, he will look for ways to avenge his wrongs by finding ways to serve.

Paul described this kind of turnaround in his second letter to the Corinthians. He had sent them a rather scorching letter, and then in the second letter he was commenting on their response to him. He had corrected some of their childish, boorish ways, and now he saw in them a whole new attitude. He wrote:

> Even if I caused you sorrow by my letter, I do not regret it. Though I did regret it—I see that my letter hurt you, but only for a little while—yet now I am happy, not because you were made sorry, but because your sorrow led you to repentance. For you became sorrowful as God intended and so were not harmed in any way by us. Godly sorrow brings repentance that leads to salvation and leaves no regret, but worldly sorrow brings death. See what this godly sorrow has produced in you: what earnestness, what eagerness to clear yourselves, what indignation, what alarm, what longing, what concern, what readiness to see justice done. At every point you have proved yourselves to be innocent in this matter. (2 Corinthians 7:8-11)

If you don't see this kind of attitude in your fool, then his repentance is not genuine. You also need to look for another aspect of the truly repentant heart: a willingness to wait. When someone is genuinely sorry for his sin, he does not push the person he has wounded to move more quickly or to take care of his own needs.

I talked with a man who had played the fool in his daughter's life by sexually abusing her for six years. When she confronted him in front of her mother, he acted very sad and very sorry. But the minute he was told that he would have to find another place to live, his response was, "Why do I have to do without my wife?" That man was not repentant.

If your fool responds to the natural consequences of his sin with complaints and conditions, then he is not committed to biblical repentance. When you hear strains of martyrdom slipping in, such as, "I only did it for you and the children" or "Everything I said was to protect you and your sister," it is probably best to keep waiting and see what the results of the "turnaround" will actually be.

I hope these answers to the questions I am most often asked about foolproofing a life are helpful to you. You are on a long, exciting, often exhausting journey. I pray that you will know new freedom, increased confidence, and an ever-growing trust in your Lord as you become a person who is "wise about what is good, and innocent about what is evil" (Romans 16:19).

ABOUT THE AUTHOR

Jan Silvious is a practical communicator of God's Word. Her passion is to teach that life in Jesus Christ is real and that in him wisdom to live an emotionally whole and spiritually vital life can be found no matter what one's circumstances are.

Keynoting for conferences has become a natural extension of her experience as a counselor with DaySpring Counseling in Chattanooga, where she worked for several years with women on the issues that cause them pain. Jan approaches each audience as if she were talking with an individual in her office. She speaks the truth of God's Word with conviction, practical application, humor, and encouragement.

Jan's other books include *Look at It This Way, Big Girls Don't Whine,* and *Smart Girls Think Twice.* She is a regular guest of the Moody Broadcasting Network on *Midday Connection* and *Prime Time America.*

She lives in Chattanooga, Tennesee, with Charlie, her husband of more than forty years.